My
Android™ Tablet

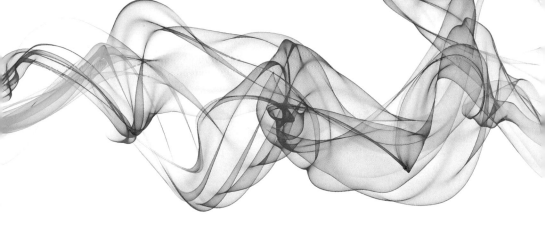

Craig James Johnston

800 East 96th Street,
Indianapolis, Indiana 46240 USA

My Android Tablet

Copyright © 2015 by Pearson Education, Inc.

ISBN-13: 978-0-7897-5368-7
ISBN-10: 0-7897-5368-5

Library of Congress Control Number: 2014952477

Printed in the United States of America

Second Printing: March 2015

Trademarks

All terms mentioned in this book that are known to be trademarks or service marks have been appropriately capitalized. Que Publishing cannot attest to the accuracy of this information. Use of a term in this book should not be regarded as affecting the validity of any trademark or service mark.

Warning and Disclaimer

Every effort has been made to make this book as complete and as accurate as possible, but no warranty or fitness is implied. The information provided is on an "as is" basis. The author and the publisher shall have neither liability nor responsibility to any person or entity with respect to any loss or damages arising from the information contained in this book.

Special Sales

For information about buying this title in bulk quantities, or for special sales opportunities (which may include electronic versions; custom cover designs; and content particular to your business, training goals, marketing focus, or branding interests), please contact our corporate sales department at corpsales@pearsoned.com or (800) 382-3419.

For government sales inquiries, please contact governmentsales@pearsoned.com.

For questions about sales outside the U.S., please contact international@pearsoned.com.

Editor-in-Chief
Greg Wiegand

Acquisitions Editor
Michelle Newcomb

Development Editor
Charlotte Kughen, The Wordsmithery LLC

Managing Editor
Kristy Hart

Senior Project Editor
Lori Lyons

Copy Editor
Apostrophe Editing Services

Senior Indexer
Cheryl Lenser

Proofreader
Debbie Williams

Technical Editor
Christian Kenyeres

Editorial Assistant
Cindy Teeters

Compositor
Bronkella Publishing

Contents at a Glance

Table of Contents

2 Audio, Video, and Movies   69

About the Author

Craig James Johnston has been involved with technology since his high school days at Glenwood High in Durban, South Africa, when his school was given some Apple][Europluses. From that moment technology captivated him, and he has owned, supported, evangelized, and written about it.

Craig has been involved in designing and supporting large-scale enterprise networks with integrated email and directory services since 1989. He has held many different IT-related positions in his career ranging from sales support engineer to mobile architect for a 40,000 smartphone infrastructure at a large bank.

In addition to designing and supporting mobile computing environments, Craig co-hosts the CrackBerry.com podcast, as well as guest hosting on other podcasts including iPhone and iPad Live podcasts. You can see Craig's previously published work in his books *Professional BlackBerry*, and *My iMovie*, plus many other books in the *My* series, including books covering BlackBerry, Palm, and Android devices.

Craig also enjoys high-horsepower, high-speed vehicles and tries very hard to keep to the speed limit while driving them.

Originally from Durban, South Africa, Craig has lived in the United Kingdom, the San Francisco Bay Area, and New Jersey, where he now lives with his wife, Karen, and a couple cats.

Craig would love to hear from you. Feel free to contact Craig about your experiences with *My Android Tablet* at http://www.CraigsBooks.info.

All comments, suggestions, and feedback are welcome, including positive and negative.

Dedication

"I love deadlines. I like the whooshing sound they make as they fly by."
—Douglas Adams

Acknowledgments

I would like to express my deepest gratitude to the following people on the *My Android Tablet* team who all worked extremely hard on this book.

My agent Carole Jelen, my acquisitions editor Michelle Newcomb, as well as technical editor Christian Kenyeres, development editor Charlotte Kughen, senior project editor Lori Lyons, copy editor San Dee Phillips, senior indexer Cheryl Lenser, compositor Tricia Bronkella, and proofreader Debbie Williams.

We Want to Hear from You!

As the reader of this book, *you* are our most important critic and commentator. We value your opinion and want to know what we're doing right, what we could do better, what areas you'd like to see us publish in, and any other words of wisdom you're willing to pass our way.

We welcome your comments. You can email or write to let us know what you did or didn't like about this book—as well as what we can do to make our books better.

Please note that we cannot help you with technical problems related to the topic of this book.

When you write, please be sure to include this book's title and author as well as your name and email address. We will carefully review your comments and share them with the author and editors who worked on the book.

Email: feedback@quepublishing.com

Mail: Que Publishing
          ATTN: Reader Feedback
          800 East 96th Street
          Indianapolis, IN 46240 USA

Reader Services

Visit our website and register this book at quepublishing.com/register for convenient access to any updates, downloads, or errata that might be available for this book.

In this chapter, you become familiar with the external features of a typical Android tablet and the basics of getting started with the Android operating system. Topics include the following:

→ Your Android tablet's external features

→ Fundamentals of Android 5.0 (Lollipop)

→ First-time setup

→ Synchronization software

Getting to Know Your Android Tablet

You can start to get to know more about your Android tablet by examining the external features, device features, and how Google's latest operating system—Android 5.0 (Lollipop)—works.

One important thing to remember about any Android tablet bearing the Nexus name is that it is a pure Android tablet with no wireless carrier or vendor modifications. This book refers to this unchanged version of Android, but where appropriate some vendor-specific information is also included.

Your Android Tablet's External Features

Becoming familiar with the external features of your Android tablet is a good place to start because you will be using them often.

Front

Front camera

Light sensor

Touchscreen

Back button

Recent Apps button

Home button

Light sensor Normally placed near the front camera, it adjusts the brightness of the screen based on the brightness of the ambient light.

Front camera Front-facing camera that you can use for video chat, taking self-portraits, and even unlocking your Android tablet using your face. Some tablets might not have a front-facing camera.

Touchscreen The Android tablet has a screen that incorporates 10-finger capacitive touch. The exact physical dimensions, technology used, and resolution of the screen differ depending on which vendor makes and sells the tablet.

Back button   Tap to go back one screen when using an application or menu. This virtual button is actually on the screen; however some tablet vendors place a touch-sensitive Back button below the screen.

Recent Apps button   Tap to see a list of recently used apps and switch between them. This virtual button is actually on the screen. Some vendors, such as Samsung, modify Android so that this virtual button is removed. These vendors normally require that you touch and hold the Home button to see recent apps.

Home button   Tap to go to the Home screen. The application that you are using continues to run in the background. This virtual button is actually on the screen; however, some vendors, such as Samsung, place an actual physical Home button below the screen.

Menu button—Some vendors, such as Samsung, keep the Menu button even though it is a hold-over from a much older version of Android. Tap the Menu button to see a context-aware menu of options based on the screen or app you are using.

Button Placement

Google creates Android, and in older versions of Android, many devices that ran Android used physical buttons and even featured trackballs for navigation. More recent versions of Android have moved the physical buttons onto the screen as virtual buttons. Android also no longer has a Menu button (virtual or not), opting for a Menu icon in each app. However some vendors, such as Samsung, have chosen to implement buttons using their own design. Samsung has chosen to keep the physical Home button on all its devices. Samsung (as well as some other vendors) also has kept the Back and Recent Apps buttons below the screen. Depending on the model of Samsung tablet you own, you may have a Recent Apps button or a Menu button. These are some variations you might see.

Back

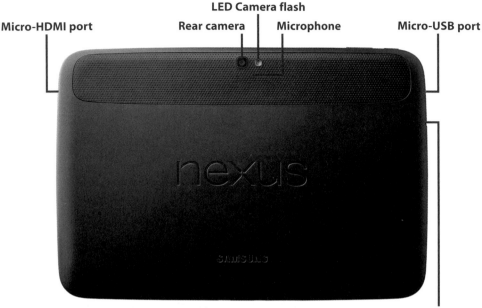

LED Camera flash

Micro-HDMI port | **Rear camera** | **Microphone** | **Micro-USB port**

3.5mm headphone jack

Micro-HDMI port Some tablets include a Micro-HDMI port that enables you to use a Micro-HDMI-to-HDMI cable to play videos from your tablet onto a television or monitor.

Microphone Used for video and audio calls (using apps such as Skype or Google Talk). The actual placement of this microphone differs between manufacturers; however, it is normally on the top edge of the tablet or on the back near the top.

3.5mm headphone jack Used with third-party headsets so that you can enjoy music and talk on the tablet. The actual placement of the headphone jack differs based on the manufacturer of the tablet.

Micro-USB port Used to synchronize your Android tablet to your desktop computer and charge it. The placement of the Micro-USB port differs based on the manufacturer of the tablet. Some manufacturers are starting to include a Micro-USB 3 port, which is slightly longer.

LED camera flash Illuminates the area when you're taking photos or recording video.

Rear camera Rear-facing camera. The exact lens type, sensor resolution, and aperture differ based on who makes and sells the tablet. Some tablets do not include a rear camera.

Other Buttons and Connectors

Docking pins

Docking pins   Use with accessories and docks to automatically start certain applications and charge your Android tablet. For example, a vehicle dock could automatically launch the Navigation app. Not all tablets include this connector, and the location of it differs based on which company manufacturers the tablet.

Volume up/ down button   **Power button**

Power button   Press once to wake your Android tablet. Press and hold for 1 second to reveal a menu of choices. The choices enable you to put your Android tablet into silent mode, airplane mode, or power it off completely. The location of the Power button differs based on the tablet manufacturer.

Volume up/down buttons   Control the audio volume on calls and while playing audio and video. The location of the volume buttons differs based on the tablet manufacturer.

Other Sensors and Radios

Your Android tablet includes a Wi-Fi (WLAN) radio for connecting to your home or office networks or to Wi-Fi hotspots in airports, coffee shops, and even on planes. It also has a Bluetooth radio for connecting Bluetooth accessories such as headsets. Some tablets may include a Near Field Communications (NFC) radio for mobile payments and swapping information between other Android devices. On the sensor front your tablet probably has an accelerometer for detecting movement, a compass for directional awareness, a gyroscope for assisting with movement detection and gaming, a Global Positioning System (GPS) for detecting where you are on the planet, and, in some cases, a Hall Sensor for detecting a magnetic field.

First-Time Setup

Before setting up your new Android tablet, it is advisable that you have a Google account. This is because your Android tablet running Android is tightly integrated into Google and enables you to store your content in the Google cloud, including any books and music you buy or movies you rent. If you do not already have a Google account, go to https://accounts.google. com on your desktop computer and sign up for one.

You Need Wi-Fi to Set Up Your Android Tablet

You need to connect to a Wi-Fi network when you set up your Android tablet.

Set Up Your Android Tablet

1. Press the Power button until you see the animation start playing.

2. Swipe up or down to change your location if needed.

3. Tap the arrow button to start the setup process.

4. Select a Wi-Fi network to connect to.

5. Type in the Wi-Fi network password.

6. Tap Connect.

7. If you have another Android device (tablet or smartphone) running Android 5.0 (Lollipop), and you want to transfer the data from it to your new tablet, follow the instructions on this screen, or tap Skip to continue.

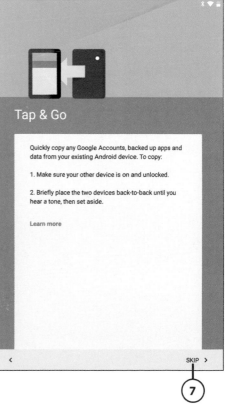

Select Wi-Fi

DukeNukem

DukeNukem 5GHz

HomeWireless

⑤　**④**　　　**⑥**

DukeNukem

Passw ....|
ord

☐ Show password

☐ Advanced options

　　　　　　CANCEL　CONNECT

Tap & Go

Quickly copy any Google Accounts, backed up apps and data from your existing Android device. To copy:

1. Make sure your other device is on and unlocked.

2. Briefly place the two devices back-to-back until you hear a tone, then set aside.

Learn more

‹　　　　　　　　　SKIP ›

⑦

8. Enter your Gmail email address if you already have a Gmail account, and tap Next.

9. Enter your Google account password.

10. Tap Next.

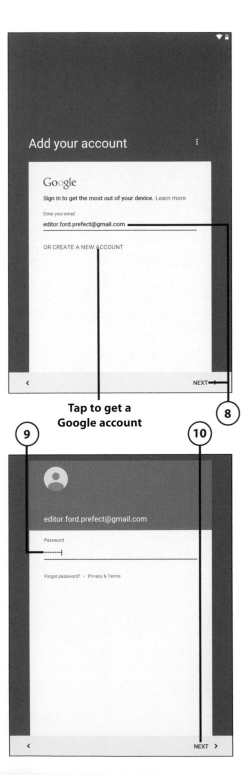

Tap to get a Google account

11. Check this box if you want to back up your tablet's data so that it can be restored to a new tablet or smartphone in the future.

12. Check this box if you are okay with Google collecting information about your geographic location at any time. Although Google keeps this information safe, if you are concerned about privacy rights, you should uncheck this box.

13. Check this box if you are okay with your tablet scanning for Wi-Fi networks even if you have the Wi-Fi radio turned off. This helps improve location accuracy.

14. Check this box if you are okay letting Google collect diagnostic information about your tablet and the apps running on it.

15. Tap Next to complete your tablet setup.

⑫ ⑪

Google services

This tablet may also receive and install updates and apps from Google, your carrier, and your tablet's manufacturer. Some apps may be downloaded and installed if you continue, and you can remove them at any time.

☑ **Back up your tablet's apps, app data, settings, and Wi-Fi passwords** using your Google Account so you can easily restore later. Learn more

☑ **Use Google's location service** to help apps determine location. This means sending anonymous location data to Google, even when no apps are running. Learn more

☑ **Help improve location services** by letting apps and services scan for Wi-Fi networks even when Wi-Fi is off.

☑ **Help improve your Android experience** by automatically sending diagnostic and usage data to Google. This information won't be used to identify you and helps us improve how our teams working on

‹   NEXT ›

⑬ ⑭   **⑮**

Extra Setup Steps for Some Tablets

Many vendors that make Android tablets modify them so that they include special services and features unique to their brand of tablets—for example, separate app stores, special cloud services that provide backup and restore services, and other unique brand-only features. Normally, these features require that you have an account with the vendor itself in addition to having your Google account. Some tablet vendors include extra apps such as Dropbox and use those services to back up your tablet or store the pictures you take with the camera. During the tablet setup, you might be asked to enter your vendor-specific account details (or create a new account) or participate in extra services such as Dropbox. It's up to you whether you want to create this account or use only your Google account.

Fundamentals of Android 5.0 (Lollipop)

Your Android tablet is run by an operating system called Android. Android was created by Google to run on any tablet or smartphone, and quite a few tablets and smartphones run on Android today. This book covers the latest version of Android, called Android 5.0 (also called Android Lollipop).

The Lock Screen

If you haven't used your Android tablet for a while, the screen goes blank to conserve battery power. Here is how to interact with the lock screen.

1. Press the Power button to wake up your Android tablet. Some tablets have a physical Home button (as discussed earlier) and in these instances, pressing the physical Home button also wakes up your tablet.

2. Swipe up anywhere on the screen to unlock your tablet.

Notifications

7:03

Thursday, November 20

Google+ Auto Backup   11/19/14
2 photos ready to share
editor.ford.prefect@gmail.com

Screenshot captured.   11/19/14
Touch to view your screenshot.

New Google+ notifications   10/26/14
Introduction to Wearable Technology and Google Glass: This.
zaphodbeeblebrox75@gmail.com   2

6 applications updated   5:58 AM
Google Play Music, Google Slides, Google Sheets, G...

USB debugging connected
Touch to disable USB debugging.

Charging (46 mins until full)

2

Swipe left to launch the Camera app

Talk to Your Tablet While It's Sleeping

As long as it's plugged into power, you can speak to your tablet and give it commands, even while it is sleeping. Just say "OK Google," and it will wake up and listen for commands. You can search your tablet or the Internet, or give commands to send an email, add reminders, and many other things. To enable this feature, go to Settings, Language & Input, Voice Input, and tap the cog icon to the right of Enhanced Google services. Then tap "OK Google" Detection, and make sure all three switches are in the on position.

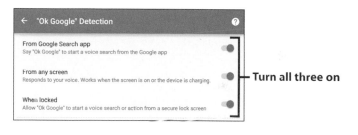

Work with Notifications on the Lock Screen

With Android 5.0 (Lollipop), you can work with notifications right on the lock screen. If you see notifications in the middle of the screen, touching one takes you straight to the app that created it. Read more about notifications later in this section.

Work with Android Settings on the Lock Screen

With Android 5.0 (Lollipop), you can work with settings (such as Airplane Mode, turning Wi-Fi on or off, and so on) right on the lock screen. To work with settings, pull down the Quick Settings bar by sliding down from the top of the screen with two fingers to view and change commonly used settings. Tap the Settings icon to see a full list of settings. Tap the user icon to log in as a different tablet user, a guest tablet user, or create a new tablet user. Tablet user is covered later in this prologue.

The Home Screen

After you unlock your Android tablet, you are presented with the middle Home screen pane. Your Android tablet typically has five Home screen panes. The Home screen panes contain application shortcuts, a Launcher icon, a Notification Bar, Shortcuts, a Favorites Tray, and widgets.

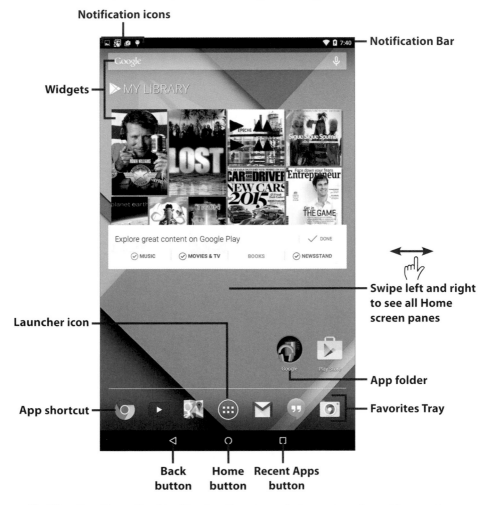

Notification icons

Notification Bar

Widgets

Swipe left and right to see all Home screen panes

Launcher icon

App folder

App shortcut

Favorites Tray

Back button   Home button   Recent Apps button

Notification Bar   The Notification Bar shows information about Bluetooth, Wi-Fi, and cellular coverage, as well as the battery level and time. The Notification Bar also serves as a place in which apps can alert or notify you using notification icons.

Notification icons   Notification icons appear in the Notification Bar when an app needs to alert or notify you of something. For example, the tablet app can show the new email icon indicating that you have new unread emails.

Working with Notifications and Quick Settings

To interact with notifications that appear in the Notification Bar, place one finger above the top of the screen and swipe down to reveal the notifications. Swipe each individual notification off the screen to the left or right to clear them one by one. Using two fingers, drag down on a notification to expand it. You can also work with settings (such as Airplane Mode or turning Wi-Fi on or off). To work with settings, tap the Quick Settings Bar to view and change commonly used settings. Tap the Settings icon to see a full list of settings. If you want to get to Quick Settings right away, use two fingers and swipe down from the top of the screen. The Quick Settings Bar will slide down, with the notifications underneath it. Swiping down to see notifications and Quick Settings works on any screen, and while running any app.

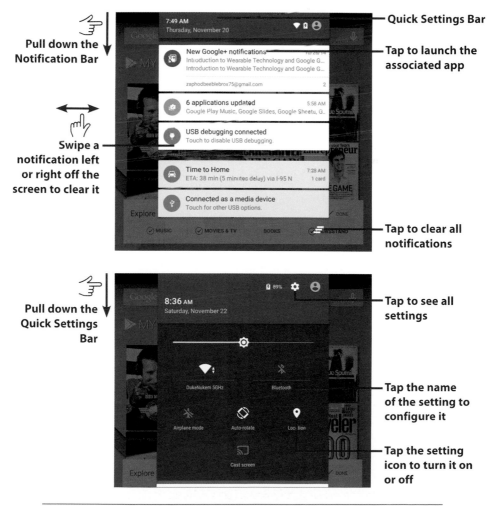

Differences Between Tablets

Some tablets modify the way that Quick Settings works. For example, when you swipe down with two fingers on a Samsung tablet, you see a lot more Quick Settings icons. To control how many you see, tap the pencil icon. To configure a setting like Bluetooth, touch and hold the setting icon. Tap the icon to turn the setting on or off.

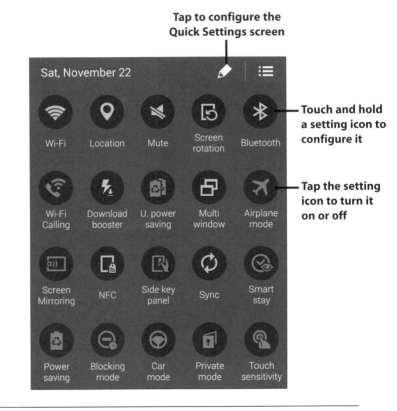

Tap to configure the Quick Settings screen

Touch and hold a setting icon to configure it

Tap the setting icon to turn it on or off

Widgets Widgets are mini apps that run right on the Home screen panes. They are specially designed to provide functionality and real-time information. An example of a widget is one that shows the current weather or provides search capability. You can move and resize widgets.

App shortcut Tapping an app shortcut launches the associated app.

Creating App Shortcuts

Tap the Launcher icon to see all your apps. Touch and hold on the app you want to make a shortcut for. After the Home screen appears, drag the app shortcut to where you want it on the Home screen, drag it to an app folder to add it to the folder, or drag it left or right off the screen to move it between Home screen panes. Release the icon to place it.

 —Touch and hold an app icon

— Drag between Home screen panes

— Drag to where you want it and release it

App folders App folders are groups of apps that you can use to organize and declutter your screen.

Creating App Folders

To create a new app folder, simply drag one app shortcut onto another one. An app folder is created automatically. To name your new app folder, tap the folder to open it, and tap Unnamed Folder to enter your custom name.

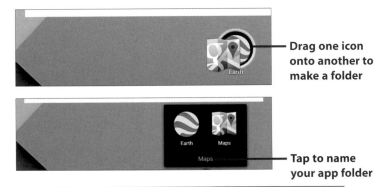

Drag one icon onto another to make a folder

Tap to name your app folder

Favorites Tray   The Favorites Tray is visible on all five Home screens. You can drag apps to the Favorites Tray so that they are available no matter which Home screen pane you are looking at. You can rearrange and move apps in the Favorites Tray.

Launcher icon   Tap to show application icons for all applications that you have installed on your Android tablet.

The System Bar

Your Android tablet running Android 5.0 (Lollipop) has no physical buttons. Instead it has an area of the screen set aside for virtual buttons. This area is called the System bar. The System bar includes the Back, Home, and Recent Apps virtual buttons.

My Tablet Doesn't Have a System Bar

Although Google's Android operating system is designed to use virtual buttons in the System bar, some tablet vendors, such as Samsung, have chosen to use physical and touch-sensitive buttons below the screen. Because the buttons are below the screen, there is no need to have a System bar. Refer to the "Button Placement" margin note earlier in this prologue for more information.

System bar

Back   Home Recent Apps
button   button   button

System bar   Reserved area of the screen where virtual buttons are displayed.

Back button   Tap to go back one screen in an app or back one step while navigating Android.

Home button   Tap to exit what you are doing and return to the Home screen. Your app continues to run in the background.

Recent Apps button   Tap to see your recently used apps, switch between them, and close them.

Using Your Touchscreen

Interacting with your Android tablet is done mostly by touching the screen—what's known as making gestures on the screen. You can tap, touch and hold, swipe, pinch, double-tap, and type.

Tap   To start an application, tap its icon. Tap a menu item to select it. Tap the letters of the onscreen keyboard to type.

Touch and hold   Touch and hold to interact with an object. For example, if you tap and hold a blank area of the Home screen, a menu pops up. If you tap and hold an icon, you can reposition it with your finger.

Drag   Dragging always starts with a tap and hold. For example, if you tap and hold the Notification Bar, you can drag it down to read all the notification messages.

Swipe or slide   Swipe or slide the screen to scroll quickly. To swipe or slide, move your finger across the screen quickly. Be careful not to tap and hold before you swipe or you will reposition something. You can also swipe to clear notifications or close apps when viewing the recent apps.

Double-tap   Double-tapping is like double-clicking a mouse on a desktop computer. Tap the screen twice in quick succession. For example, you can double-tap a web page to zoom in to part of that page.

Pinch   To zoom in and out of images and pages, place your thumb and fore-finger on the screen. Pinch them together to zoom out or spread them apart (unpinch) to zoom in. Applications such as Browser, Photos, and Maps support pinching.

Rotate the screen   If you rotate your Android tablet from an upright position to being on its left or right side, the screen switches from portrait view to landscape view. Most applications honor the screen orientation. The Home screens and Launcher do not.

Using Your Keyboard

Your Android tablet has a virtual (onscreen) keyboard for those times when you need to enter text. You might be a little wary of a keyboard that has no physical keys, but you will be pleasantly surprised at how well it works.

Most apps automatically show the keyboard when you need to enter text. If the keyboard does not appear, tap the area where you want to type and the keyboard slides up ready for use.

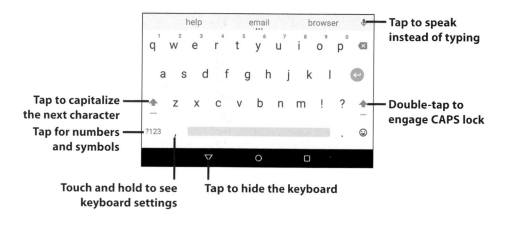

Tap to speak instead of typing

Tap to capitalize the next character

Double-tap to engage CAPS lock

Tap for numbers and symbols

Touch and hold to see keyboard settings

Tap to hide the keyboard

Keyboard Quick Tips

If you are typing an email address or a website address, the keyboard shows a button labeled .COM. If you tap it, you type .COM, but if you touch and hold it, you can choose between .EDU, .GOV, .ORG, and .NET. If you tap and hold the Return key, the cursor jumps to the next field. This is useful if you fill out forms on a website or move between fields in an app. If you touch and hold the comma key, you can change the language and keyboard settings.

Using the virtual keyboard as you type, your Android tablet makes word suggestions. Think of this as similar to the spell checker you would see in a word processor. Your Android tablet uses a dictionary of words to guess what you are typing. If the word you were going to type is highlighted, tap the space or period to select it. If you can see the word in the list but it is not highlighted, tap the word to select it.

Tap to select an alternative suggested word

List of suggested words

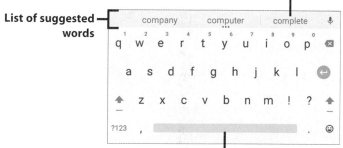

Tap space to accept the suggested word in the middle

Add Your Word

If you type a word that you know is correct, you can add it to your personal dictionary so that the next time you type it, your Android tablet won't try to correct it. To do this, after you type the word—but before you tap space—you'll notice that your word is underlined. Tap on the underlined word, and your word appears in the middle of the suggested words area. Tap the word to add it to your personal dictionary. Tap it once more to complete the action.

First, tap your word to add it to the dictionary.

My company uses StreetTalk

| street talk | StreetTalk | street tall |

Next, tap the word as it appears here.

My company uses StreetTalk

StreetTalk   ←Touch again to save

Tap your word again to complete the save

To make the next letter you type a capital letter, tap the Shift key. To make all letters capitals (or CAPS), double-tap the Shift key to engage CAPS Lock. Tap Shift again to disengage CAPS Lock.

To type numbers or symbols, tap the Symbols key.

When on the Numbers and Symbols screen, tap the Symbols key to see extra symbols. Tap the ABC key to return to the regular keyboard.

```
1  2  3  4  5  6  7  8  9  0   ⌫

   @  #  $  %  &  -  +  (  )   ⏎

~[<  \  =  *  "  '  :  ;  !  ?  ~[<    Tap to see
                                       more symbols

ABC  ,  _  [          ]  /  .  ☺
```

Tap to return to letters

Tap to see more symbols

To enter an accented character, touch and hold any vowel or the C, N, or S keys. A small window opens enabling you to select an accented or alternative character. Slide your finger over the accented character, and lift your finger to type it.

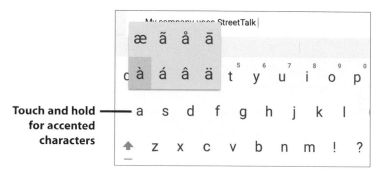

Touch and hold for accented characters

To reveal other alternative characters, tap and hold any other letter, number, or symbol.

Want a Larger Keyboard?

Turn your Android tablet sideways to switch to a landscape keyboard. The landscape keyboard has larger keys and is easier to type on.

Landscape keyboard

Dictation: Speak Instead of Typing

Your Android tablet can turn your voice into text. It uses Google's speech recognition service, which means that you must have a connection to the cellular network or a Wi-Fi network to use it.

1. Tap the microphone key.

2. Wait until you see Speak Now, and then start saying what you want to be typed. You can speak the punctuation by saying "comma," "question mark," "exclamation mark," or "exclamation point."

3. Stop speaking to finish dictation.

Tap to select a different dictation language

Tap to cancel voice dictation

Swipe to Type

Instead of typing on the keyboard in the traditional way by tapping each letter individually, you can swipe over the letters in one continuous movement. This is called Gesture Typing. It is enabled by default; to use it, just start swiping your finger over the letters of the word you want to type. As you swipe your finger, you see a trail following your finger. Lift your finger after each word. To add a space, swipe over the space bar, or just start the next word and let the keyboard add the space for you. To type a double letter (as in the word "pool"), loop around that letter on the keyboard.

Edit Text

After you enter text, you can edit it by cutting, copying, or pasting the text. Here is how to select and copy text, and then paste over a word with the copied text.

1. While you are typing, tap and hold a word you want to copy. The word highlights in blue, and you see end markers on either side of the word.

2. Slide the blue end markers until you have selected all the text you want to copy. In this example, we just need the one word.

3. Tap to copy the text. You can also cut the text. This example demonstrates copying text.

4. Touch and hold the word you want to paste over.

5. Tap Paste.

Tap to select all text ①

Tap to cut the text

③

← Text selection   ⊡ SELECT ALL   ✂ CUT   ⧉ COPY

From   editor.ford.prefect@gmail.com   ⌄

To   ⌄

First email on my new tablet

Hi Craig.

I'm enjoying my new portable so far.
What are you doing for dinner tomorrow night? I'd like to show it to you.

Ford.

②

⑤

← Text selection   ⊡ SELECT ALL   ✂ CUT   ⧉ COPY   ⧉ PASTE

From   editor.ford.prefect@gmail.com   ⌄

To   ⌄

First email on my new tablet

Hi Craig.   **PASTE**

I'm enjoying my new portable so far.
What are you doing for dinner tomorrow night? I'd like to show it to you.

Ford.

④

Simpler Copy/Paste

You might want to just copy some text and paste it somewhere else, instead of pasting it over a word. To do this, after you have copied the text, tap once in the text area, and move the single blue marker to where you want to paste the text. Tap the blue marker again, and tap Paste.

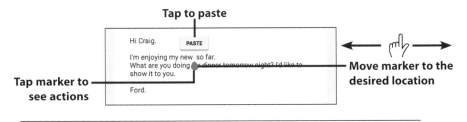

Tap to paste

Tap marker to see actions

Move marker to the desired location

Menus

Your Android tablet has two types of menus: App menus and Context menus. Let's go over what each one does.

Most applications have a Menu icon, which enables you to make changes or take actions within that application. The Menu icon should always appear in the top-right corner of an app; however, it can sometimes appear in the System bar next to the Recent Apps button or elsewhere in the app. Remember that some tablets have a physical Menu button below the screen and might not have the onscreen Menu icon.

Tap the Menu icon to reveal the App menu

New tab

New incognito tab

Bookmarks

Recent tabs

History

Share...

Print...

A context menu applies to an item on the screen. If you tap and hold something on the screen (in this example, a link on a web page), a context menu appears. The items on the context menu differ based on the type of object you tapped.

Touch and hold a link to reveal the link context menu

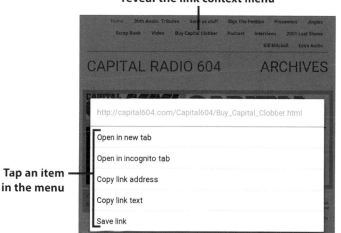

Tap an item in the menu

Switch Between Apps

Your Android tablet has an icon called the Recent Apps icon. This icon is always on the System bar at the bottom of your screen. You can use this icon to switch between apps, close apps, and force them to quit if they have stopped responding.

1. Tap the Recent Apps icon.

2. Scroll up and down the list of recent apps.

3. Swipe an app left or right off the screen to close it.

4. Tap and hold an app's icon to reveal the app's information screen.

Tapping the X icon also closes the app

5. Tap to force an app to close if it has stopped responding.

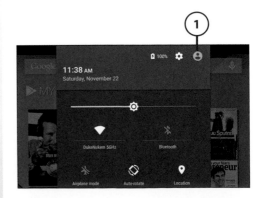

My Tablet Doesn't Have a Recent Apps Button

Tablets made by some vendors such as Samsung remove the Recent Apps button and replace it with a Menu button. In these cases, press and hold the Home button to reveal the Recent Apps screen.

Setting Up Multiple Users on Your Tablet

Your Android tablet has the capability to support multiple users. This enables you to share your tablet among co-workers, family members, or friends, with each person having his own unique login, apps, photos, videos, and settings. Your tablet can support up to eight users. Some tablet vendors do not allow this option.

Add a New Tablet User

Tablet users can have their own apps, photos, videos, wallpapers, and do anything on the tablet with the exception of removing other users and factory resetting the tablet. To add other users, the original owner of the tablet must be logged in and needs to use the following steps. The user being added should also be present at the time the new user profile is created.

1. Pull down the Quick Settings pane, and tap the user icon.

2. Tap Add User.

3. Tap OK.

4. Tap Set Up Now.

5. Hand the tablet to the person who will be setting up her account. She can now follow the steps in the section called "First-Time Setup," earlier in this chapter.

How to Switch Between Tablet Users

To switch between tablet users, pull down the Quick Settings Bar on the lock screen, Home screen, or while running any app, and tap the user icon. Tap the user you want to switch to.

Tap the user icon to switch users

Tap a user to switch to

Add a Tablet Guest User

A tablet guest user can use the tablet like a regular user; however, the user's information is not permanently saved. There can only be one guest account, and it can either be reused by the same guest, or wiped for a new guest.

1. Pull down the Quick Settings pane, and tap the user icon.

2. Tap Add Guest.

3. Hand the tablet to the guest. No setup is required.

Continue as a Guest or Start Over

If you previously added a guest user and allowed someone to use it, the guest account will remain untouched until your guest wants to use it again. If the same person wants to continue where they left off, when they switch to the guest user they will be asked to either start over or continue. If they tap Continue, their guest session will continue where it left off. However, if you are allowing a new person to use the guest user, he must tap Start Over to wipe the previous guest session and start fresh.

Tap to start as   **Tap to continue as**
a new guest   **the previous guest**

>>>*Go Further*

LET YOUR CHILDREN USE YOUR TABLET SAFELY

When you add a new user, the user has his own Google account and full access to all apps that he installs while he is logged in to the tablet. A restricted profile is a copy of your own login profile but with apps and content restricted. You can imagine using restricted profiles for your children who may not have their own Google account and who should not have access to all apps. By creating a restricted profile, you can decide which apps and content the person may access, but you don't have to worry about having to set up a whole new user on your tablet. Restricted profiles appear like new users but actually function under your user account with restrictions in place. To add a restricted profile, go into Settings, tap Users, tap Add user or Profile, and tap Restricted Profile. If you haven't already, you will be asked to set a screen lock. This is to protect your account so nobody can just switch back to it. After you set your screen lock, you set up the restricted profile.

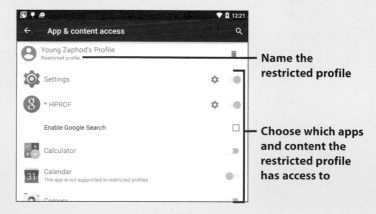

Name the restricted profile

Choose which apps and content the restricted profile has access to

Installing Synchronization Software

Because your Android tablet is tightly integrated with Google and its services, all media that you purchase on your tablet is stored in the Google cloud and accessible anywhere and anytime. However, you might have a lot of music on your computer already that you need to copy to your Google cloud, so you need to install the Google Music Manager software or the Android File Transfer app for your PC or Mac to copy any file back and forth.

Install Android File Transfer (Apple Mac OS X)

You need only the Android File Transfer app when using an Android tablet on an Apple Mac running OS X, and only if you think you want to drag files to and from your tablet using Finder.

1. From your Mac, browse to http://www.android.com/filetransfer/ and download the Android File Transfer app.

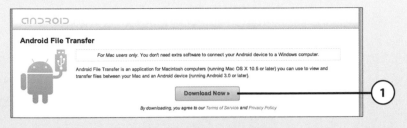

2. Click the downloads icon to reveal your downloaded files.

3. Double-click the androidfiletransfer.dmg file in your Safari Downloads.

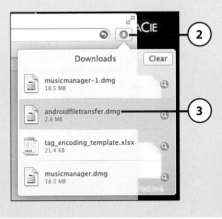

4. Drag the green Android to the Applications shortcut to install the app.

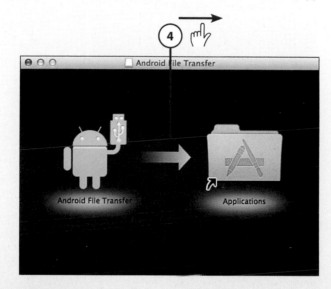

Install Google Music Manager (Apple Mac)

Don't install Google Music Manager unless you plan to upload files from your computer to the Google Music cloud.

1. Visit https://play.google.com/music/listen#manager_pl from your desktop web browser, and log in to your Google account if prompted.

2. Click Download Music Manager.

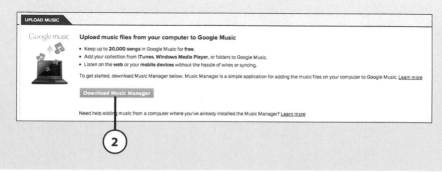

3. Click the downloads icon to reveal your downloaded files.

4. Double-click the musicmanager.dmg file in your Safari Downloads.

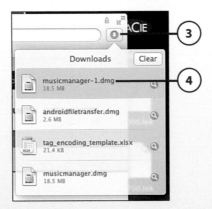

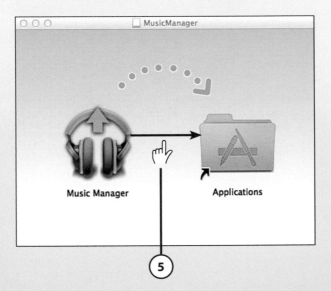

5. Drag the Music Manager icon to the Applications shortcut to install the app.

6. Double-click the Music Manager icon in the Applications folder.

7. Skip to the "Configure Music Manager" section later in the prologue to complete the installation.

Install Google Music Manager (Windows)

Don't install Google Music Manager unless you plan to upload files from your computer to the Google Music cloud.

1. Visit https://music.google.com/music/listen#manager_pl from your desktop web browser, and log in to your Google account if prompted.

2. Click Continue to download Music Manager.

3. Double-click the musicmanagerinstaller app in your Downloads folder, and then follow the steps in the next section.

Configure Music Manager (Windows and Apple Mac)

1. Click Continue.

2. Enter your Google (Gmail) email address.

3. Enter your Google (Gmail) password.

4. Click Continue.

5. Choose where you keep your music.

6. Click Continue.

7. Choose whether to upload all your music or just some of your playlists. Remember that you can upload only 20,000 songs for free. Skip to Step 12 if you choose to upload all music.

8. Check if you want to also upload podcasts.

9. Click Continue.

10. Select one or more playlists of music.

11. Click Continue.

12. Choose whether you want to automatically upload any new music that is added to your computer.

13. Click Continue, and your files start uploading.

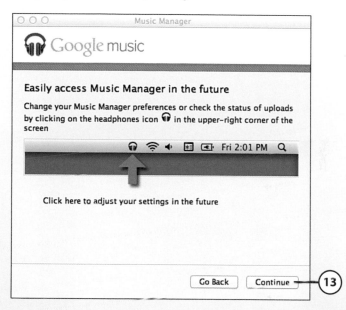

14. Click Close.

Choose what to show

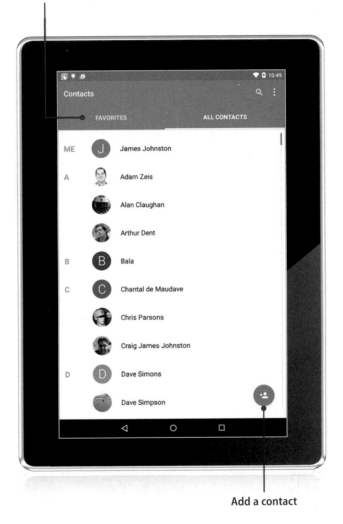

Add a contact

In this chapter, you discover the app that's your Android tablet's hub of all communication: Contacts. You learn how to add and synchronize contacts, join duplicate contacts together, and even how to add a contact to your Home screen. Topics include the following:

→ Importing contacts

→ Adding contacts

→ Synchronizing contacts

→ Creating favorite contacts

Contacts

On the Android tablet, the Contacts app is sometimes called People. You can synchronize your contacts from many online sites such as Facebook and Gmail, so as your friends change their Facebook profile pictures, their pictures on your Android tablet change, too.

Adding Accounts

Before you look around the Contacts application, try adding some accounts to synchronize contacts from. You already added your Google account when you set up your Android tablet in the Prologue.

Adding Facebook, Twitter, LinkedIn, and Other Accounts

To add accounts for your online services, such as Facebook, Twitter, LinkedIn, and so on, install the apps for those services from Google Play. See Chapter 8, "Working with Android Applications," for information about how to install apps. After you have installed the apps and you have logged into them, visit the "Accounts" section in Settings and add a new account as shown in the following sections to see new accounts for each online service.

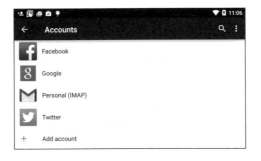

Add a Work Email Account

Your Android tablet can synchronize your contacts from your work email account as long as your company uses Microsoft Exchange or an email gateway that supports Microsoft ActiveSync (such as Lotus Traveler for Lotus Domino/Notes email systems). It might be useful to keep your work and personal contacts on one mobile device instead of carrying two devices.

Mobile Device Management (MDM) and Containers

More and more companies are starting to use Mobile Device Management (MDM) systems to manage mobile devices. The following steps describe a situation in which your company does not use an MDM system and you are manually adding your work account to your Android tablet. If your company does use an MDM system, the setup of your work account will be handled automatically. With Android, many companies also deploy a Container or Dual Persona app. This Dual Persona app provides a secure area in which your email, contacts, and calendar reside. When a Container or Dual Persona is used, you use the Dual Persona app for email, contacts, and calendar instead of the built-in Android apps. Some examples of these Container or Dual Persona apps are Good Technology, Divide, and AirWatch Inbox. Samsung also provides one called KNOX on some models of its tablets and smartphones.

Finding Add Account on a Samsung Tablet

Samsung heavily modifies Android on their tablets. To add a new account on a Samsung tablet, first tap Settings. On the Settings screen, tap General in the Menu bar. You then see the Add account icon. From that point onward, the steps should be the same.

1. From the Home screen, pull down the Quick Settings Bar.

2. Tap the Settings icon.

3. Tap Accounts in the Personal section.

4. Tap Add Account.

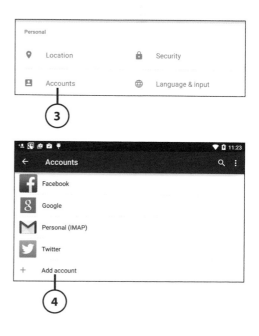

5. Tap Exchange. Sometimes this account type is called Corporate.

6. Enter your full corporate email address and tap Next.

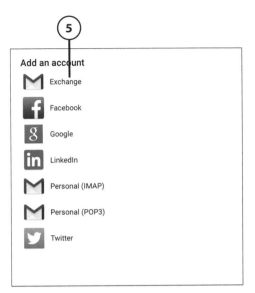

7. Enter your corporate network password.

8. Tap the Next icon.

What Is a Client Certificate?

Your company might require that you use a certificate as a method of authenticating to the email system, instead of using your username and password. There are advantages to doing this; for example, when your password changes, it doesn't stop your Android tablet from receiving email.

9. Enter your company's mail server name, and then tap the Next icon at the bottom of the screen.

Error Adding Account? Guess the Server

Your Android tablet tries to work out some information about your company's ActiveSync setup. If it can't, you are prompted to enter the ActiveSync server name manually (as described in Step 9). If you don't know what it is, you can try guessing it. If, for example, your email address is dsimons@allhitradio.com, the ActiveSync server is most probably webmail.allhitradio.com or autodiscover@allhitradio.com. If this doesn't work, ask your email administrator.

10. Tap OK to agree that your mail administrator might impose security restrictions on your Android tablet if you proceed.

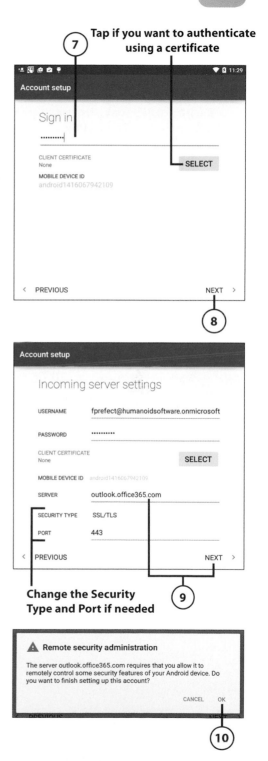

Tap if you want to authenticate using a certificate

Change the Security Type and Port if needed

Remote Security Administration

Remote Security Administration is another way of saying that when you activate your Android tablet against your work email servers, your email administrator can add restrictions to your tablet. The restrictions can include forcing a lock screen password, imposing the need for a strong password, and requiring how many letters and numbers the password must be. Your email administrator also has the power to remotely wipe your Android tablet so that it is put back to factory defaults, which is what the administrator might do if you lose your tablet or it is stolen.

11. Tap to choose how often your corporate email is delivered to your Android tablet. Automatic means that as it arrives in your Inbox at work, it is delivered to your tablet. You can set it to Manual, which means that your work email is delivered only when you open the Email app on your tablet. You can also set the delivery frequency from every 5 minutes to every hour.

12. Tap to choose how many days in the past email is synchronized to your Android tablet or set it to All to synchronize all email in your Inbox.

13. Tap to enable or disable being notified when new email arrives from your corporate Inbox.

14. Tap to enable or disable synchronizing your corporate contacts to your Android tablet.

15. Tap to enable or disable synchronizing your corporate calendar to your Android tablet.

16. Tap to enable or disable synchronizing your corporate email to your Android tablet.

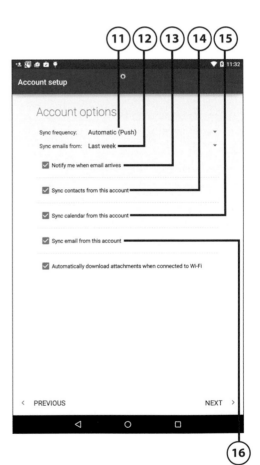

17. Tap to enable or disable automatically downloading email attachments when your Android tablet is connected to a Wi-Fi network.

What to Synchronize

You might decide that you don't want to synchronize all your work information to your Android tablet. You might decide to just synchronize email but not the calendar, or maybe just the calendar but not the contacts and email. Unchecking these boxes enables you to choose the information you don't want to synchronize. You can go back into the account settings and change it later if you change your mind.

18. Tap the Next icon.

19. Tap Activate to agree to the restrictions that are about to be imposed by your administrator on your tablet.

Account setup

Account options

Sync frequency: Automatic (Push)

Sync emails from: Last week

☑ Notify me when email arrives

☑ Sync contacts from this account

☑ Sync calendar from this account

☑ Sync email from this account

☑ Automatically download attachments when connected to Wi-Fi

< PREVIOUS   NEXT >

(17)   (18)

Activate device administrator?

M   Gmail

The server outlook.office365.com requires that you allow it to remotely control some security features of your Android device.

Activating this administrator will allow the app Gmail to perform the following operations:

Erase all data
Erase the tablet's data without warning by performing a factory data reset.

Set password rules
Control the length and the characters allowed in screen-unlock passwords.

Monitor screen-unlock attempts
Monitor the number of incorrect passwords typed when unlocking the screen, and lock the tablet or erase all the tablet's data if too many incorrect passwords are typed.

Lock the screen
Control how and when the screen locks.

CANCEL   ACTIVATE

(19)

20. Enter a name for this email account. Use something meaningful that describes the purpose of the account such as **Work Email**.

21. Tap the Next icon to complete your work email setup.

Remove an Account

To remove an account, under the Accounts section in Settings, tap the account to be removed. For account types that can have multiple accounts (such as Corporate and Google), tap the account again on the next screen to show its sync settings. Tap the Menu icon on the top right of the screen and tap Remove Account.

Account setup

Your account is set up and email is on its way!

Give this account a name (optional)

Work Email

NEXT >

⑳   ㉑

Navigating Contacts

The People app actually has three screens. The middle one you see shows your list of contacts, but there are two others that have specific functions.

1. Tap the Contacts icon.

2. Tap to add a new contact.

3. Tap to search for a contact.

4. Tap the Menu icon to change the settings for the Contacts app, manage accounts, import or export contacts, and choose which contacts to display.

5. Tap to see only favorite contacts.

6. Tap a contact to view or edit it.

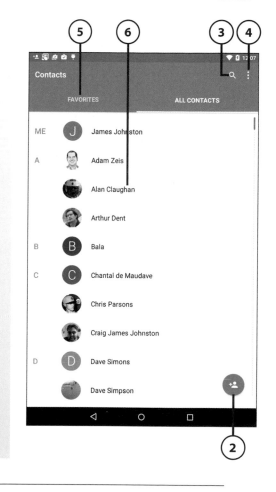

Mark a Contact as a Favorite

To mark a contact as a favorite, while you have the contact's information open, tap the star icon to the left of the edit icon.

Tap to mark as a favorite

Edit a Contact

Sometimes you need to make changes to a contact or add additional information to it.

1. Tap the contact to open the contact record.

2. Tap the Edit icon.

3. Tap the down arrow icon to enter a middle name, name prefix, and name suffix.

4. Tap the X next to a field to delete it.

5. Tap to change the field subcategory. In this example, tapping Work enables you to change the email subcategory from Work to Home to indicate that this is the contact's Home email address.

6. Tap Add New to add a new field in a specific category. In this example, tapping Add New enables you to add a new email address.

7. Tap to put the contact in a contact group. You can use a default contact group of family, friends, co-workers, or you can create a group.

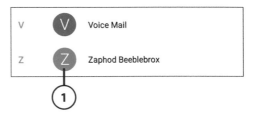

8. Tap to add a new field to the contact's contact card. New fields could be phone numbers, IM (Instant Messaging) address, notes, nickname, website, a special date (such as a birthday or anniversary), your relationship to the contact, and even an Internet phone number (or SIP number).

9. Tap the check mark to save your changes.

Add a Contact Photo

The contact photo is normally added automatically when a social network account is linked to a contact. However, you might want to manually add a picture or change the current picture.

1. Tap the Contact.

2. Tap the Edit icon.

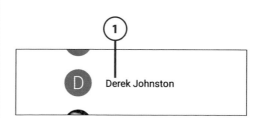

3. Tap the contact photo placeholder or, if there is already a photo, tap the photo.

4. Tap to add a photo already saved on your Android tablet.

Take a Picture

If you don't already have a photo you want to use, you can take a new photo by tapping the Take Photo option.

5. Tap the photo you want to use.

Take a photo with the camera ③

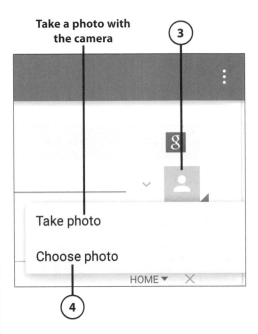

Take photo

Choose photo

④

⑤

6. Drag the cropping box to select the area of the photo you want to use as the contact photo.

7. Drag the outside of the cropping box to expand or contract it.

8. Tap Done to save the cropped photo as the contact photo.

Adding and Managing Contacts

As you add contacts to your work email account or Google account, those contacts are synchronized to your Android tablet automatically. When you reply to or forward emails on your tablet to an email address that is not in your Contacts, those email addresses are automatically added to the contact list or merged into an existing contact with the same name. You can also add contacts to your Android tablet directly.

Add Contacts from an Email

To manually add a contact from an email, first open the email client (either email or Gmail) and then open an email message. See Chapter 4, "Email," for more on how to work with email.

1. Tap the blank contact picture to the left of the sender's name.

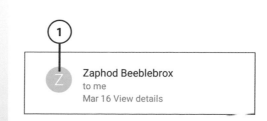

2. Tap OK to add the sender's email address to your contacts.

Add "zbeeblebrox@capital604.com" to contacts?

Cancel   OK

3. Choose an existing contact that you want to add the email address to if you already have the contact in your list and want to add an additional email address to it. If you do this, skip the rest of the steps.

← Choose a contact

Create new contact

A   Adam Zeis

Alan Claughan

4. Tap Create New Contact to create a new contact and add this email address to it.

5. Tap to choose which account you want to add this contact to (if you have more than one account).

6. Enter additional information about your new contact.

7. Tap the check mark to save the new contact.

✓ Add new contact

Google contact
editor.ford.prefect@gmail.com

Name

Add organization

PHONE

Phone   MOBILE ▼

EMAIL

zbeeblebrox@capital604.com   HOME ▼ ✕

Add new

ADDRESS

Add a Contact Manually

1. Tap the Contacts icon.

2. Tap to add a new contact.

3. Tap to select which account the new contact is being added to. For example, you might want to add the new contact to your work email account instead of your personal account.

4. Enter the person's full name.

5. Tap to choose a contact picture.

6. Tap to enter a middle name, name prefix and suffix, and phonetic names.

7. Enter information including phone numbers, email address, and events.

8. Tap the check mark to save the new contact.

Add a Contact from a vCard

vCards are files that can be attached to emails. These vCards contain a virtual business card that you can import into the People app as a new contact. Use the following steps to add a new contact from a vCard.

1. Tap the attachment that has the .vcf extension.

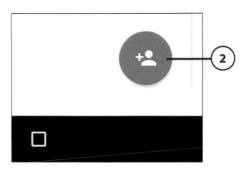

2. Tap to select which account you want to add the new contact to. For example, you might want to add the new contact to your work email account instead of your personal account.

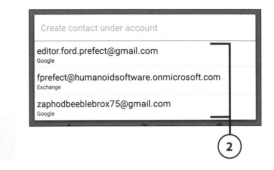

Sharing a Contact

To share a contact, tap the Menu icon and tap Share. The exact list of methods to share a contact is determined by the apps you have installed on your tablet—in general, however, you should be able to share a contact via Android Beam (or if you are using a Samsung Tablet and sharing the contact with another Samsung users, S-Beam), Bluetooth, save it to your Google Drive, or send it via the Email app or Gmail app.

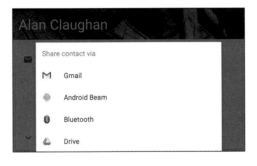

>>>*Go Further*

WHAT IS NEAR FIELD COMMUNICATIONS (NFC)?

Your Android tablet might have an NFC radio and antenna built in. When you hold either another device with built-in NFC or an NFC tag close to the back cover, the NFC antenna and radio reads the data. You can learn more about NFC at http://en.wikipedia.org/wiki/Near_field_communication.

Beam a Contact

If you want to send a contact via NFC, you can use the Beaming feature, which is built in to your Android tablet. To beam a contact, make sure the contact is selected, and bring the other person's NFC-enabled smartphone or tablet back to back with your tablet. After you hear a tone, you see the screen zoom out. Touch the screen to send the contact card to the other device.

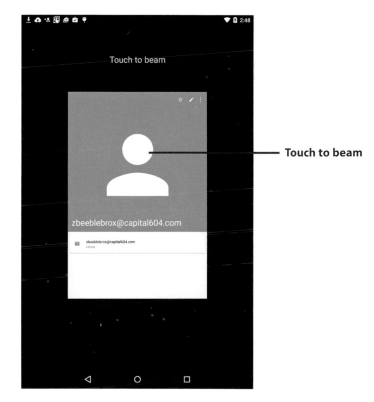

Touch to beam

Beam from a Samsung Tablet

Samsung smartphones and tablets support Android Beam, but they also use a Samsung-specific version of it called S-Beam. If you are using an Android tablet and are trying to beam a contact to a non-Samsung smartphone or tablet, it may not work unless you go into Settings and disable S-Beam. After S-Beam is disabled, your Samsung tablet will revert to using the standard Android Beam functionality. The same goes for someone using a Samsung smartphone and tablet and attempting to beam a contact to you.

Customize Contacts Settings

There are a couple settings that you might want to customize for the Contacts app, such as choosing the contact list display order and whether to display contacts using their first names first or last names first.

1. Tap the Menu icon.

2. Tap Settings.

3. Tap to choose the sort order of the list of contacts in the People app. You can sort the list by first name or last name.

4. Tap to choose how each contact is displayed. You can display contacts by first name first or last name first.

5. Tap the arrow to save the settings.

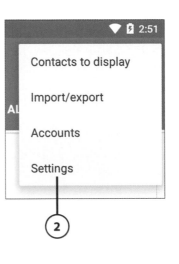

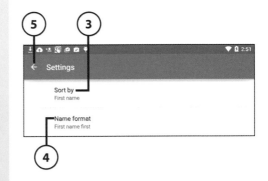

Contact Groups

You can create contact groups—such as Friends, Family, Inner Circle—and then divide your contacts among them. This can be useful if you don't want to search through all your contacts to find a family member. Instead you can just touch the Family group and see only family members. The following steps show you how to manage what group(s) a particular contact belongs to.

1. Tap a contact.

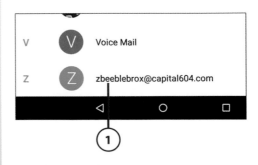

2. Tap the Edit icon.

3. Tap Group Name to manage what groups this contact belongs to.

4. Select one or more groups to add the contact to.

5. Tap outside of the group selection area after you make your changes.

6. Tap the check mark to save the changes to the contact.

Tap to create a new group

It's Not All Good

You Can't Use Groups

Even though you can add contacts to groups using the standard Android apps such as Gmail and Contacts, you cannot actually use the groups for anything. For example, you'd think it would be useful to send an email to a group, and then all members of that group would receive the email. It's a great idea, but it's not possible. Even within the Contacts app, you cannot search a group name. The only thing you can use groups for is for refining the Contacts display, which is covered in the next section. Hopefully, this will change in the future.

Choose Contacts to Display

You can choose to hide certain contact groups from the main contacts display; for example, you can choose to show only contacts from your corporate account or only certain groups of contacts from your Google account.

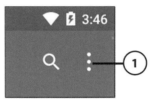

1. Tap the Menu icon.

2. Tap Contacts to Display.

3. Tap to show all contacts from all accounts.

4. Tap an account to show only contacts from that account.

5. Tap to customize which groups in each account are displayed.

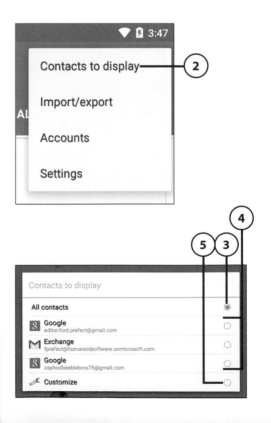

6. Tap to expand an account to see subgroups of contacts.

7. Tap to select or deselect a subgroup of contacts. In this example, we have chosen to only show contacts who are in the Family group.

8. Tap OK to save the settings.

Define custom view

editor.ford.prefect@gmail.com
Google

fprefect@humanoidsoftware.onmicrosoft.com
Exchange

zaphodbeeblebrox75@gmail.com
Google

Cancel   OK

Define custom view

editor.ford.prefect@gmail.com
Google

My Contacts ☐

Starred in Android ☐

Friends ☐

Family ☑

Cancel   OK

Joining and Separating Contacts

As you add contacts to your Android tablet, they are automatically merged if the new contact name matches a name that's already stored. Sometimes, you need to manually join contacts together or separate them if your Android tablet has joined them in error.

Join Contacts Manually

1. Tap the contact that you want to join a contact to.

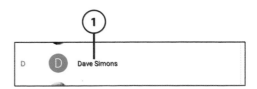

D   D   Dave Simons

2. Tap the Edit icon.

3. Tap the Menu icon.

4. Tap Join.

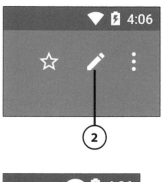

Separate

Join

Discard changes

Delete

5. Tap the contact you want to join with. The Contacts app suggests contacts, but you can also search for them.

6. Tap the check mark to complete the join process.

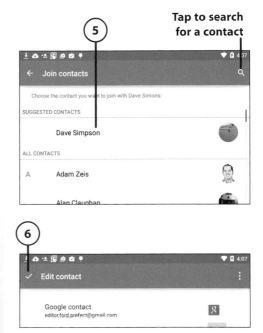

Tap to search for a contact

Separate Contacts

When you follow these steps to separate contacts that have either been automatically or manually joined, all previous joins will be separate—including automatic ones that the Contacts app does when it sees duplicate contacts.

1. Tap the contact that you want to separate.

2. Tap the Edit icon.

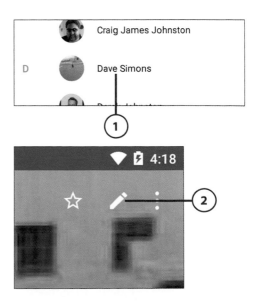

3. Tap the Menu icon.

4. Tap Separate.

5. Tap OK to separate the contacts.

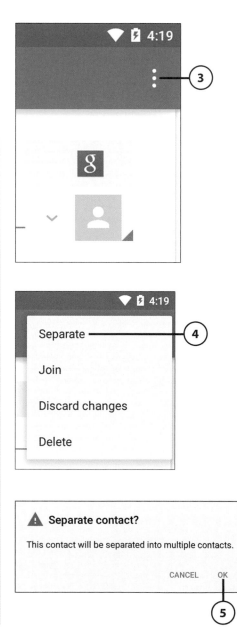

Adding a Contact to Your Home Screen

If you communicate with some contacts so much that you are constantly opening and closing the Contacts app, a quicker solution might be to add a shortcut to the contacts on the Home screen.

1. Tap the contact you want to add to your Home screen.

2. Tap the Menu icon.

3. Tap Place on Home Screen. A shortcut to the contact is placed on an available spot on the Home screen.

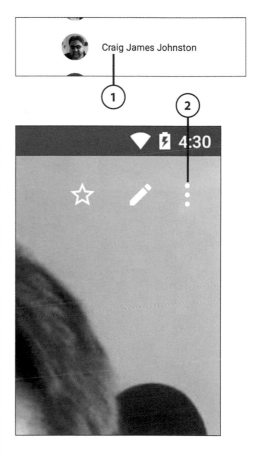

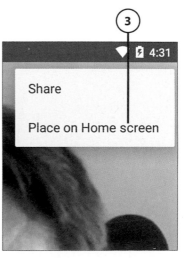

Reposition or Remove the Shortcut

After you have a contact shortcut on your Home screen, you can reposition it by touching and holding it, and while you are still holding it, drag it around the screen, or off the sides of the screen to move it between the Home screen panes. Release the shortcut to complete the reposition. To remove the contact shortcut, touch and hold it; then drag it up to where you see the word Remove and release it.

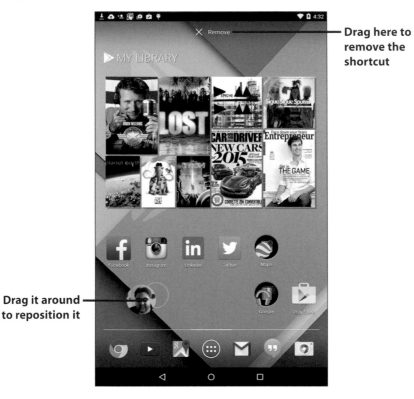

Drag here to remove the shortcut

Drag it around to reposition it

>>>Go Further

IMPORTING AND EXPORTING CONTACTS

You can import any vCards that you have saved to your Android tablet's internal storage. You can also export your entire contact list to your Android tablet's internal storage or share that entire contact list via Bluetooth, email, Gmail, or, if you have any NFC tag writer software installed, write it to an NFC tag. To access the import/export functions, tap the Menu icon and tap Import/Export. When you export contacts to storage, you can find them in /mnt/sdcard when browsing your Android tablet from your Mac or PC.

Contacts to display

Import/export ——————— **Tap to import or export contacts**

Accounts

Settings

Tap to import vCards

Import/export contacts

Import from storage

Export to storage ————

Share visible contacts

Tap to share the selected contact   **Tap to export one or more contacts to storage**

Tap to find movies   Tap to find TV shows

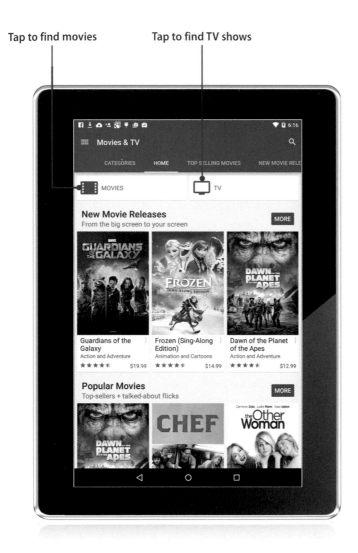

In this chapter, you discover your Android tablet's audio and video capabilities, including how your Android tablet plays video and music and how you can synchronize audio and video from your desktop computer or Google Play Music. Topics include the following:

→ Using Google Play Music for music
→ Using the Photos app for pictures and video
→ Renting movies with Google Play
→ Working with YouTube

Audio, Video, and Movies

Your Android tablet has strong multimedia capabilities. The large screen enables you to turn your Android tablet sideways to enjoy a video in its original 16:9 ratio. You can also use your Android tablet to search YouTube, watch videos, and even upload videos to YouTube right from your tablet. Android fully embraces the cloud, which enables you to store your music collection on Google's servers so that you can access it anywhere.

Music

Your Android tablet ships with a Google Play Music app, which enables you to listen to music stored on your tablet as well as from your collection in the Google Play Music cloud. Using Google Play you can also find and buy more music.

Find Music

The best place to discover and find music is in the Google Play store.

1. Tap the Google Play icon on the Home screen.

2. Tap to see only what's offered in the music category.

3. Tap to sort music by genre.

4. Tap to see top-selling albums.

5. Tap to see new releases.

6. Tap to see top-selling songs.

7. Tap to search for music.

8. Scroll down to see more music.

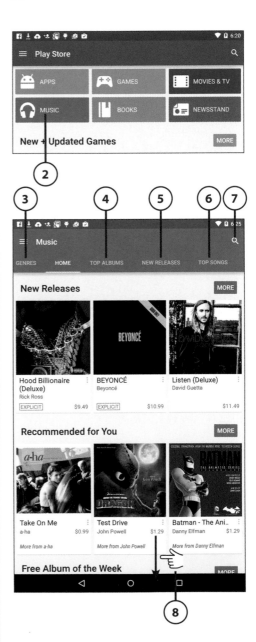

Purchase Music

After you find a song or album you're interested in, follow these steps to purchase it. Remember that when you purchase music, it does not download to your tablet; instead, it's automatically added to your Google Cloud.

Free Music

Sometimes songs are offered for free. If a song is offered for free, you see the word FREE instead of a price for the song. Even though the song is free, you still need to follow the steps outlined in this section; however, the price is reflected as 0.

Adding a Payment Method

Before you purchase music, you need to make sure that you have a way to pay for it. To do that, you need to add a payment method to your Google Wallet account. To do this on your desktop computer, browse to http://wallet.google.com and log in. Click Payment Methods, and if you do not already have a valid payment method, click Add A Payment Method. Enter one of your valid debit or credit cards.

1. Tap the price to the right of the song title if you want to purchase the song, or album if you want to purchase the entire album.

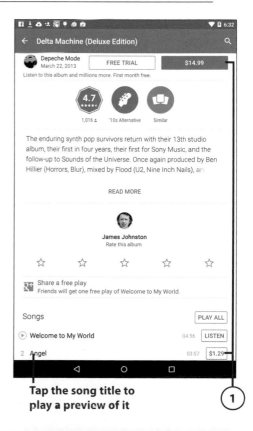

Tap the song title to play a preview of it

2. Tap Buy.

3. Tap Listen to hear your song after
    the purchase is complete. The
    song opens in the Play Music app
    and streams from your Google
    Cloud account over the air.

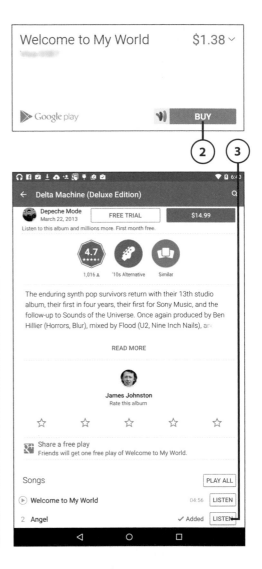

It's Not All Good

Cloud and Data Usage

Although the idea of cloud storage (where your music is stored on Google
computers as opposed to your Android tablet) is beneficial, it does mean that
anytime you listen to your music collection it is streamed over the Wi-Fi or
cellular data network. If you are not connected to Wi-Fi or cellular data, you
cannot access and listen to your music. You can plan for a no-coverage situation by keeping some music on your tablet. See the section titled "Listening
to Music with No Wireless Coverage" later in this chapter.

Add Your Existing Music to Google Play Music

You can upload as many as 20,000 songs from Apple iTunes, Microsoft Windows Media Player, or music stored in folders on your computer for free to your Google Play Music cloud account by using the Google Music Manager app on your desktop computer. If you haven't already installed Google Music Manager, please follow the steps in the "Installing Google Music Manager" section in the Prologue.

1. Click (right-click for Windows) the Google Music Manager icon. (This icon is in the Mac Menu Bar at the top of the screen or in the Windows Task Bar at the bottom of the screen.)

2. Choose Preferences. (Use the Options command if you are on Windows.)

3. Click to upload new songs you've added since you last used Music Manager to upload music.

4. Click to upload the remainder of songs that have not yet uploaded to Google Play Music.

5. Click to upload songs in certain playlists. This works only for iTunes or for Windows Media Player.

6. Choose the playlists to upload.

7. Click Upload after you have made your selections.

8. Click to allow Google Music Manager to automatically upload new songs added.

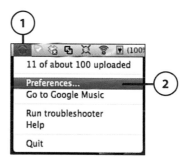

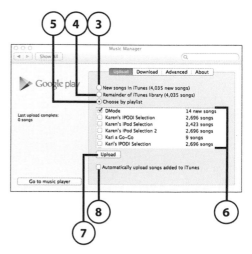

Automatic Upload

If you choose to have your music uploaded automatically in Step 8, Google Music Manager continually monitors Apple iTunes, Microsoft Windows Media Player, or your Music folders to see when you add music. If it finds new music, Google Music Manager automatically uploads it. (After you install Google Music Manager, the software is always running on your computer.)

What if I Don't Have iTunes or Windows Media Player?

If you don't have or don't use Apple iTunes or Microsoft Windows Media Player to store and play your music, Google Music Manager can upload music from folders on your computer. Click the Advanced Tab, click Change, and select either Music Folder (to use the folder on your computer called Music) or Other Folders (so you can choose folders where you store your music). Click Add Folder to add a new folder to the list.

Select to choose other folders

Can I Download Music to My Computer?

You can download your entire music collection from Google Play Music to your computer, or just download music you have purchased on your Android tablet by clicking the Download tab in Google Music Manager Preferences.

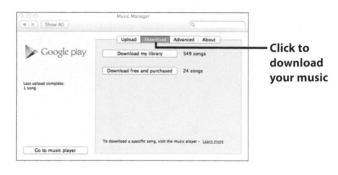

Click to download your music

Use the Music App

Now that you have purchased some music and/or synchronized it from your computer, it's time to take a look at the Google Play Music app on your Android tablet.

1. Tap the Play Music icon on the Home screen.

What Is Listen Now?

Listen Now is the first screen you are presented with when you launch the Music app. This view is dynamically created based on what music you have uploaded, purchased, and listened to. It contains your music, music accessible via All Access, and radio stations. All Access is a subscription service that enables you to access a vast collection of music. As you scroll around the Listen Now screens, you are not visually cued as to what music is on All Access, and what music you have uploaded or purchased; everything is just seamlessly put together. For a free 30-day trial of All Access, use your computer to visit http://play.google.com/about/music/allaccess/#/.

2. Scroll down to explore the Listen Now screen.

3. Tap to search for music. This includes music loaded on your tablet, stored in the Google Cloud, available in All Access (if you subscribe to it), and playing on online radio stations.

4. Swipe in from the left side of the screen to see a menu.

5. Tap to return to the Listen Now screen.

6. Tap to see only music in your music library. This is all music you have purchased and uploaded.

7. Tap to see playlists that you have created and playlists that have been automatically created for you.

8. Tap to browse and create Instant Mixes (previously called Radio Stations) that will play your music. We will cover Instant Mixes later in this chapter.

9. Tap to explore music that is available to play and purchase.

10. Tap to switch between showing only music that is already downloaded to your tablet, or showing music no matter where it resides, including in your Google Cloud account.

11. Tap to change the Google Play Music app settings.

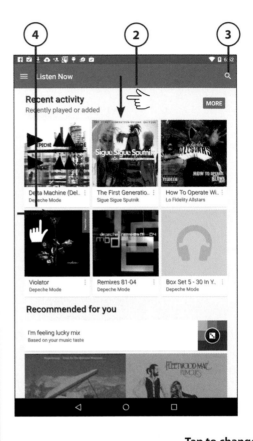

Tap to change the Google account to use if you have more than one

Work with My Library

My Library shows all music you have uploaded from your computer or purchased in the Google Play Store.

Swipe Between Views
As you follow the steps in this task, instead of tapping the view titles, such as Albums and Artists, you can swipe left and right to move between these views.

1. After tapping My Library as shown in Step 6 of the "Use the Music App" task, tap Genres to filter the view by genre. Tap an album name to reveal songs on that album and then touch a song to play it.

2. Tap Artists to filter the view by artist. Tap an artist's name to reveal songs by that artist, and then touch a song to play it.

3. Tap Albums to filter the view by album title. Touch an album name to reveal songs on that album, and then touch a song to play it.

4. Tap Songs to filter the view by song title. This shows all songs by all artists. Touch a song to play it.

5. Tap to search for music in your collection.

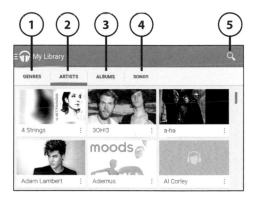

What's Playing
If you are currently playing music, the bottom of the Music app shows the information about the song and allows you to pause it or jump backward and forward through the playlist.

Work with Playlists

Playlists can be created automatically for you, such as playlists of songs you have given a thumbs up to or music you last added to your library, but you can also manually create playlists.

1. After tapping Playlists as shown in Step 7 of the "Use the Music App" task, tap to search for music by song or artist. This does not let you search for a playlist.

2. Tap the Menu icon at the bottom of a playlist to see a list of actions.

3. Tap to shuffle the songs in the playlist.

4. Tap to play the next song in the playlist.

5. Tap to add the playlist and all its songs to the queue of music currently playing.

6. Tap to download the playlist (and all the songs in the playlist) to your tablet rather than storing it only in the Google Cloud. This enables you to play the songs even when your tablet cannot connect to a Wi-Fi or cellular network.

How to Create or Add to a Playlist

You can create a playlist from any song or add a song to any playlist. Tap the Menu icon to the right of the song and tap Add to Playlist. When the list of playlists appear, either tap an existing playlist or tap New Playlist and provide a playlist name.

Tap the Menu icon   **Create new playlist**   **Add to existing playlist**

Add/create playlist

Edit or Delete Playlists

1. Tap the playlist you want to edit or delete.

2. Swipe a song left or right off the screen to remove it from the playlist.

3. Reposition songs in the playlist by dragging them up and down using the song anchor.

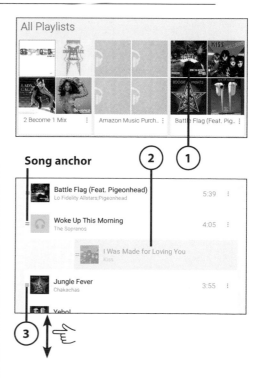

Song anchor

4. Tap the Menu icon to see more actions.

5. Tap to delete the playlist.

Battle Flag (Feat. Pigeonhead) Mix

My playlist
25 songs

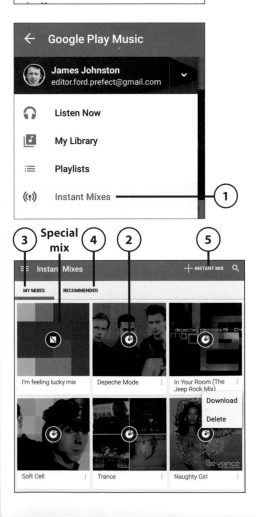

Shuffle

Play next

Add to queue

Add to playlist

Delete

Instant Mixes

Instant Mixes (previously called Radio Stations) are like channels that play music based on artist, genre, or some other shared criterion.

1. Swipe in from the left of the screen and tap Instant Mixes.

2. Tap a mix's thumbnail to start playing that Instant Mix.

3. Tap to see mixes that you have created.

4. Tap to see a list of mixes that are generated based on what music you have purchased and listened to in the past.

5. Tap to add your own new Instant Mix.

Google Play Music

James Johnston
editor.ford.prefect@gmail.com

Listen Now

My Library

Playlists

Instant Mixes

Special mix

Instant Mixes   + INSTANT MIX

MY MIXES   RECOMMENDED

I'm feeling lucky mix   Depeche Mode   In Your Room (The Jeep Rock Mix)

Download

Delete

Soft Cell   Trance   Naughty Girl

Create Your Own Instant Mixes

You can create your own Instant Mixes based on an artist, song title, or genre. After you create a mix, it plays music from the artist or song you selected, but it also plays other similar songs.

1. Type the name of a song, artist, album, or music genre.

2. Tap a mix that matches your search. This example uses the artist Tony Finger. The mix should start playing immediately.

3. Tap the music queue icon to view and edit the list of songs queued up to play.

4. Swipe a song left or right off the screen to remove it from the mix.

5. Reposition a song in the queue by dragging it up or down by the song anchor.

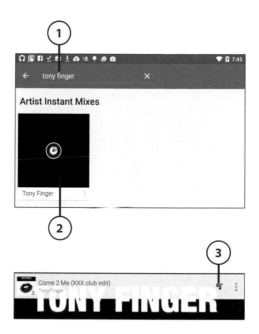

Song anchor

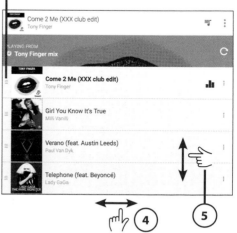

Control Playback

While your music is playing, you have some control over how a song plays and the selection of music that is queued to be played.

1. Tap to jump to the previous song in the album, playlist, or mix.

2. Tap to jump to the next song in the album, playlist, or mix.

3. Tap to pause the song. The button turns into the Play button when a song is paused. Tap again to resume playing a paused song.

4. Tap to indicate that you like the song. The Google Play Music app adds the song to the Thumbs Up playlist.

5. Tap to indicate that you do not like the song.

6. Tap the song name up to reveal the album art and more options.

7. Tap to enable or disable song shuffling. When Shuffle is enabled, songs in the current playlist or album are randomly played. The Shuffle icon is not available when you are playing an Instant Mix.

8. Tap to enable repeating. Tap once to repeat all songs; tap again to repeat the current song only; tap again to disable repeating. The repeating icon is not available when you are playing an Instant Mix.

9. Drag right and left to skip forward and backward through the song.

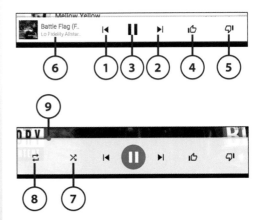

No repeating   **Repeat all songs**   **Repeat current song**

10. Tap to see and manage the list of songs in the album, playlist, or radio station.

11. Tap the Menu icon to see more options.

12. Tap to make a new Instant Mix based on the song.

13. Tap to create a playlist and add the current song to it or add the song to an existing playlist.

14. Tap to show all songs by the artist.

15. Tap to show all albums by the artist.

16. Tap to share the link to the song on social media such as Facebook, Google+, or Twitter, but also via email and SMS.

17. Tap to clear the queue of songs you made earlier and stop playing the current song. If you didn't make a queue, the current song stops playing.

18. Tap to save the Now Playing queue if you made any changes to it.

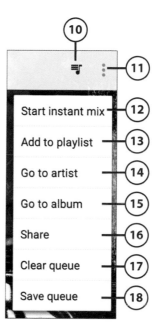

What Does Start Instant Mix Do?

If you are playing a song and choose the Start Instant Mix option, the Google Play Music app creates a new Instant Mix and adds songs to it that are similar to the one you are currently playing. The name of the mix becomes the name of the current song.

What Is the Queue?

As you see in Step 17, you can clear the queue, but what is the queue? Essentially, the queue is the Now Playing queue, a dynamic playlist that you can add songs to so that they are queued up to play one after the other. To add music to the queue, tap the Menu icon to the right of a song, playlist, or album and choose Add to Queue. This puts the song at the bottom of the current Now Playing queue. To have that song play as the next song in the queue, choose Play Next.

Work and Listen to Music

You don't have to keep the Google Play Music app open while you play music, you can switch back to the Home screen and run any other app while you still have the ability to control the music. The following steps work from the Home screen while running any app, or from the lock screen.

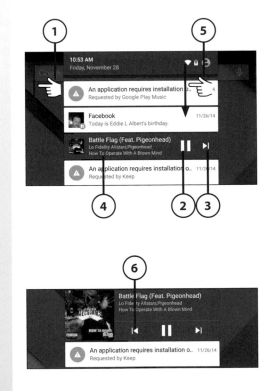

1. While on any screen, pull down the Notification Bar. If you are on the lock screen, you can skip Step 1 because notifications are always visible in the middle of the screen.

2. Tap to pause the song.

3. Tap to jump to the next song in the list, album, or playlist.

4. Tap the song title to open the Google Play Music app for more control.

5. Use two fingers and swipe down on the music control to expand it.

6. Tap to jump to the previous song in the list, album, or playlist.

Listen to Music with No Wireless Coverage

As established earlier in the chapter, if you utilize Google Play Music to store your music in the Google Cloud, when you play that music on your Android tablet, it is actually streaming over the Wi-Fi or cellular data network. If you know that you are going to be in an area without coverage but still want to listen to your music, follow these steps.

1. Tap the Download icon while viewing an album, song, or playlist.

2. The Download icon indicates the progress of the download. The amount of orange on the icon shows the progress of the download. The down arrow changes to a check mark when the download has completed.

Download progress   **Download complete**

Change Google Play Music Settings

1. Swipe in from the left of the screen to show the menu.

2. Tap Settings.

James Johnston
editor.ford.prefect@gmail.com

Listen Now

My Library

Playlists

Instant Mixes

Shop   1

Downloaded only

Settings   2

Help

Send feedback

3. Tap to change the Google account being used for Google Play Music. You can also add a new Google account to be used with the Play Music app.

4. Tap to manually refresh the list of music shown on your Android tablet.

5. Tap to subscribe to Google's All Access plan, which gives you access to their 30 million song collection anytime. Tap to cancel your monthly All Access subscription, if you have one.

6. Tap to manage the devices you use to access your music. Google allows up to ten devices.

7. Tap to enable or disable blocking explicit songs when listening to Instant Mixes.

8. Tap to enable or disable caching of streamed music. When this is enabled, music you listen to is temporarily stored on your Android tablet, so if you play one of the songs again, it plays it straight from memory.

9. Tap to enable or disable automatically caching music when you have your tablet charging and connected to a Wi-Fi network. This setting refers to music you have chosen to store locally on your tablet.

10. Tap to clear the local music cache. This removes all music you have previously chosen to be stored locally.

11. Tap to see the download queue. When you choose to make music available offline, that music is queued for download. You can see the download progress here.

12. Tap to manage the audio equalizer settings.

Adjust the Equalizer

The Google Play Music app has a Graphic Equalizer that enables you to select preset audio configurations or use your own. Tap Equalizer in the Settings screen and use the following steps to use or adjust the Equalizer.

1. Tap to turn the Equalizer on and off.

2. Tap to select from a list of preset Equalizer settings such as Dance, Hip Hop, and many more.

3. Drag the frequency response sliders to enhance or deemphasize certain frequencies.

4. Drag the slider to adjust the bass boost. The Bass Boost setting is only available when you are using headphones.

5. Drag the slider to adjust the surround sound effect, which helps the music sound like it's all around as opposed to just in your two ears.

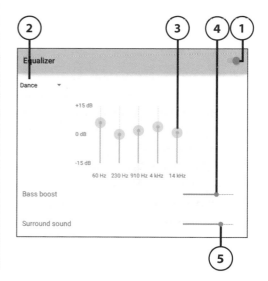

>>>*Go Further*

SYNCHRONIZE MUSIC AND OTHER MEDIA USING A CABLE

If for some reason you don't want to make use of Google Play Music or you can't because you live in a country where Google Play Music is not supported, you can synchronize music and other media using a cable (and sometimes over Wi-Fi). A great way to do this is to download an app called doubleTwist. doubleTwist has been providing media synchronization for many tablets for a while now, and the product is very mature. Head to http://doubleTwist.com to download the Windows or Mac version, and then visit the Google Play app store to download the Android app companion.

>>>*Go Further*

BEAMING MUSIC BETWEEN ANDROID DEVICES

If you know someone with an Android smartphone or tablet that has an NFC chip, you should be able to beam music to them. In theory, you should be able to send music to the other NFC-enabled device. As of the writing of this book, however, there seems to be a glitch preventing this from working correctly. Refer to the notes at the end of the section "Add a Contact from a vCard" in Chapter 1 for information on beaming.

Recording Videos with the Camera Application

The Camera application enables you to take pictures and record video. This chapter covers the video-recording feature of the Camera app. Read Chapter 13, "Taking Pictures," to get information on using the Camera app to take pictures (including Panorama and Photo Spheres).

Record Video

1. Tap to launch the Camera app.

2. Swipe in from the left of the screen to see the Camera options.

3. Tap the video icon to select the video camera mode.

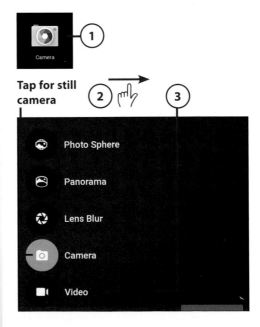

4. Tap to start recording video. Tap the icon again to stop recording.

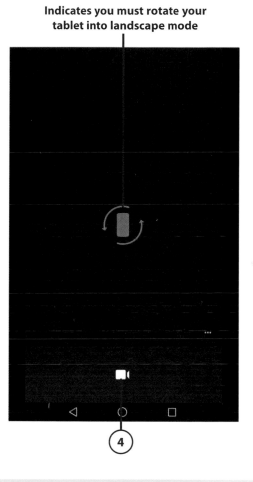

Indicates you must rotate your tablet into landscape mode

>>>Go Further

TAKING PICTURES WHILE RECORDING VIDEO

While you are recording video, you can still take pictures. To take a picture while recording video, tap the screen. Each time you tap on the screen, that frame of video is stored as a picture.

Change Video Settings

Before you record a video, you can change some settings that can alter how the video is recorded or configure it to record Time Lapse video.

1. Tap the Menu icon.

2. Tap to turn the grid pattern on or off. The grid pattern is seen only in the view finder view to help you line objects up in the shot; it does not appear on your final video.

3. Tap to switch between the front-facing and rear-facing cameras (if your tablet has both cameras).

4. Tap anywhere on the screen to close the settings.

5. Swipe in from the left of the screen.

6. Tap the Settings icon.

7. Tap to enable or disable storing your current geographic location with the video that you record.

8. Tap Advanced to enable or disable Manual Exposure. This feature only works when using the still camera mode, not video recording.

9. Tap to change the format of video recorded by the rear-facing or front-facing cameras.

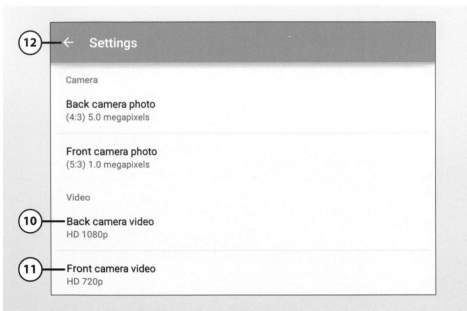

10. Tap to select the format of the video for the rear-facing camera. You can choose 1080p High Definition, 720p High Definition, or 480p Standard Definition.

11. Tap to select the format of the video for the front-facing camera. You can choose 720p High Definition, 480p Standard Definition, or a low-quality CIF format, which is 325×288 pixels.

12. Tap to return to the main camera Settings screen.

Play Videos

If you have personal videos you have recorded or people have sent you, here is how to find them and play them.

1. Tap the Photos icon to launch the Photos app.

2. Swipe in from the left of the screen to see the list of photos and videos in different locations.

3. Tap a video to open it.

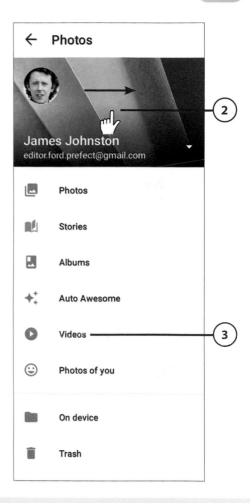

>>>*Go Further*

WHERE ARE ALL MY PHOTOS AND VIDEOS STORED?

When you open the Photos app, you'll notice that in addition to allowing you to view photos and videos on your device, it shows you a lot of other options; so what are they? If you tap Photos you see all photos and videos on your device and also ones that have previously been copied to your Google Cloud account from this and all other devices you own. If you tap Stories you access a feature of Google+ that creates stories from photos and videos that have previously been copied to your Google+ Cloud account. Tapping Albums shows you all albums on your device and in the Google+ Cloud. Tapping Auto Awesome shows you any photos and videos that have been automatically backed up to your Google Cloud account and turned into little movies. You can also manually create them. Tapping Videos shows you only videos on your device and in your Google Cloud account.

4. Tap to edit the video. This feature does not work right now.

5. Tap to delete the video.

6. Tap to share the video on YouTube; on social media including Facebook, Instagram, Google+; via Beam; via Bluetooth; or via email.

7. Tap to start playing the video.

8. Tap the screen while the video is playing to reveal the video controls.

9. Tap to pause or unpause the video.

10. Drag the slider to quickly skip forward and backward.

11. Tap to skip back 5 seconds.

12. Tap to skip forward 5 seconds.

13. Rotate your Android tablet sideways to allow the video to fill the screen.

Share Videos

You can share videos with people from the Photos app. The list of methods of sharing is dependent on the applications you have installed on your Android tablet. Many sharing methods require that you already have an account on the service you want to share on, including YouTube, Google+, Instagram, Facebook, and Path.

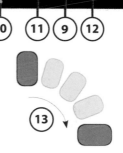

1. Touch and hold the video you want to share. You see a check mark on the video indicating that it is selected.

2. Tap additional videos you want to share if you want to share more than one.

3. Tap the Share icon to see all the ways you can share the video(s). The list of choices is dependent on the apps you have installed.

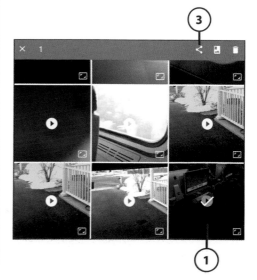

4. Tap to send the video via Bluetooth. This allows you to send the video to another device (of any kind) using Bluetooth.

5. Tap to share the video on YouTube. This allows you to upload the video to your YouTube account.

6. Tap to share the video on Google+.

7. Tap to share the video with specific people you know on Google+.

8. Tap to share the video with specific Google+ Circles.

9. Tap to share the video publicly on Google+.

10. Tap to email this video using Gmail.

11. Tap to upload the video to your Google Drive account.

12. Tap to share the video on the Instagram photo-sharing social network.

13. Tap to share with another person using Android Beam.

14. Tap to share the video on Facebook social network.

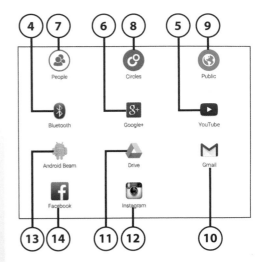

Bluetooth Sharing Might Fail

Many phones and tablets do not accept incoming Bluetooth files, but devices like computers do. Even on computers, the recipient must configure her Bluetooth configuration to accept incoming files.

Uploading or Sharing Multiple Videos

You can share or upload multiple videos at the same time, instead of one by one. After you touch and hold a video, touch more videos to add them to your list. When you select more than one video to share, however, the option to share on Facebook is disabled because you can only upload videos to Facebook one at a time. After you reduce your list of videos to share to only one video, the Facebook sharing option returns.

Delete Videos

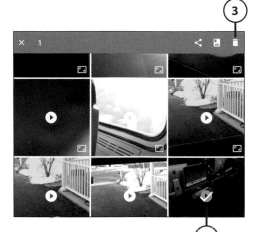

1. Touch and hold the video you want to delete.

2. Tap additional videos or photos if you'd like to delete more than one file at a time.

3. Tap the trash icon to delete the video(s).

Undeleting a Video

After you delete a video, you have 6 seconds to change your mind and undo the delete. Within 6 seconds, tap the Undo button to restore your deleted video(s).

Tap to undo your last delete

Change Photos App Settings

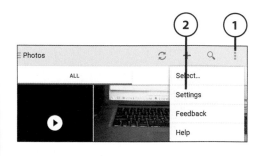

1. Tap the Menu icon in the Photos app.

2. Tap Settings.

3. Tap to change your Google account Auto Backup settings. Auto Backup automatically makes backup copies of your photos and videos to your Google+ account. They remain private and cannot be seen by others.

4. Tap to turn Auto Backup on or off.

5. Tap to change the Google account used for Auto Backup, if you have more than one account.

6. Tap to change the size of the photos that are uploaded. You can choose Standard or Full. Full size is the untouched, full resolution photo, whereas standard is a greatly reduced quality photo meant for quick sharing.

7. Tap to purchase more storage if your free storage is starting to fill up.

8. Tap to select whether to back up photos only when on Wi-Fi (and not with your cellular data connection). This option is only available for tablets that have cellular data capabilities.

9. Tap to select whether to back up videos only when on Wi-Fi (and not with your cellular data connection). This option is only available for tablets that have cellular data capabilities.

10. Tap to indicate whether it's okay to back up photos and videos while you are roaming on cellular data outside your home area. This option is only available for tablets that have cellular data capabilities.

11. Tap to select whether you want to back up your photos and videos only when your tablet is charging.

12. Tap to back up all photos and videos right now.

13. Tap to save your changes and return to the main Photos settings screen.

← Auto Backup

ACTIVE ACCOUNT

James Johnston
editor.ford.prefect@gmail.com
14.7 GB available

BACKUP STORAGE

Photo size
Full size

Get more storage
Purchase additional storage for full-size photos

BACKUP SETTINGS

Back up photos
Only when there is a Wi-Fi connection available

Back up videos
Only when there is a Wi-Fi connection available

Roaming
Back up photos & videos when roaming on a data network

While charging only
Back up photos & videos only when a charger is connected

Back up all
Back up all photos & videos now (if connection settings allow)

14. Tap to change your Google account settings for Photos.

15. Tap to choose whether the Photos app should show any photos and videos that you have stored in your Google Drive.

16. Tap to choose whether you want the Photos app to show the geographic location of where newly uploaded photos and videos were taken. The accuracy of that geographic location is set in the next step.

17. Tap to change how accurately your geographic location is reported when you take photos or videos.

18. Tap to choose whether you want your photos and videos automatically enhanced when they are backed up to Google. If enabled, Google automatically modifies your photos to make them look better.

19. Tap to choose whether Google can automatically create Auto Awesome images, movies, and stories using your photos and videos that are backed up. The Auto Awesome images, movies, and stories are only viewable by you unless you choose to share them with others.

20. Tap to choose whether you want to use this tablet to create Auto Awesome images, movies, and stories, instead of relying on the Google servers.

21. Tap to choose whether you want Google to prompt your friends to tag you in photos it can see that you are in.

22. Tap to save your changes and return to the main Photos settings screen.

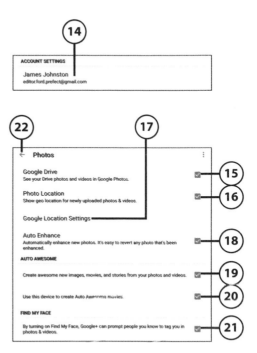

Changing How Your Tablet Determines Your Location

When you tap Google Location Settings, you can choose High Accuracy, which uses GPS, mobile networks, and nearby Wi-Fi networks to determine your location; Battery Saving, which uses only nearby Wi-Fi networks and mobile networks to determine your location; or Device Only, which uses only the GPS chip in your tablet to determine your location.

My Tablet Has the Gallery App

Android tablets used to ship with the Gallery app. This app handled all photos and video on the tablet, but was replaced by the Photos app. While Google has moved away from the Gallery app (in fact you cannot find it in the Google Play store anymore), some tablet vendors who heavily modify Android (like Samsung for example) still ship their tablets with a modified version of the Gallery app. They do this because they have integrated certain vendor-specific features into the Gallery app. The Gallery app has many of the same functions as the Photos app, so the steps you see for the Photos app will work for the Gallery app.

Movies and TV Shows

Google Play enables you to rent and purchase movies. (Most movies are available only as rentals.) You can also buy TV shows—even whole season passes of TV shows.

Buy and Rent Movies

As with music, when you buy or rent movies, they remain in the Google Cloud and stream to your tablet when you want to watch them.

1. Tap to launch Google Play.

2. Tap Movies & TV.

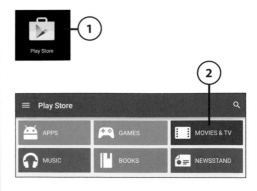

3. Scroll through the movie options, or use the Search icon to look for a specific title. Tap a movie title when you find one you want to watch.

4. Tap to see a trailer of the movie.

5. Tap to expand the synopsis.

6. Scroll down to see all information about the movie, including other viewers' reviews and ratings. You can also add your review and rating. If you see a red tomato icon, this means that the Rotten Tomatoes score is included in the reviews.

7. Tap to add the movie to your Wishlist.

8. Tap to buy the movie in either standard definition (SD) or high definition (HD).

9. Tap to rent the movie in either standard definition (SD) or high definition (HD).

Adding a Payment Method

Before you purchase or rent movies, you need to make sure that you have a way to pay for it. To do that, you need to add a payment method to your Google Wallet account. To do this on your desktop computer, browse to http://wallet. google.com and log in. Click Payment Methods, and if you do not already have a valid payment method, click Add A Payment Method. Enter one of your valid debit or credit cards.

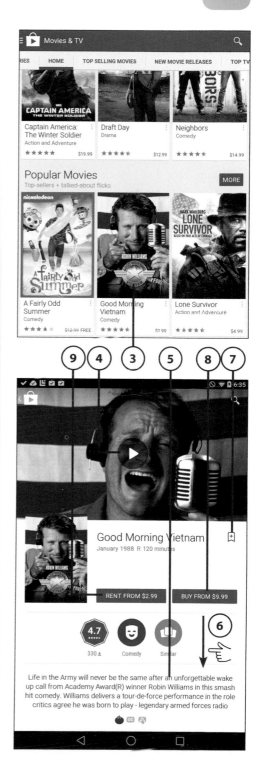

10. Tap to accept and buy or rent the movie. This example is about buying the movie.

11. Tap to first download the movie to your tablet so that you can watch it when you are not in Wi-Fi or cellular data coverage. If you purchased an HD version of the movie, you are asked whether you want to download the SD or HD version. (The HD version is a larger file.)

12. Tap to start watching the movie. This streams the movie to your tablet from the Google Cloud.

Movie Download Progress

If you choose to download the movie you rented or purchased because you know you want to watch it when you will be out of Wi-Fi or cellular data coverage (on a plane for example), you can see the progress of the movie download right on the screen. Wait until it shows Downloaded before you move out of Wi-Fi or cellular data coverage. You can also pull down the Notification Bar to see the progress of your download. To cancel the movie download, tap the push pin icon.

Download progress

Buy TV Shows

As with music and movies, when you buy TV shows, they remain in the Google Cloud and stream to your tablet when you want to watch them.

1. Tap to launch Google Play.

2. Tap Movies & TV.

3. After browsing the available TV shows or searching for a specific show, tap a show title.

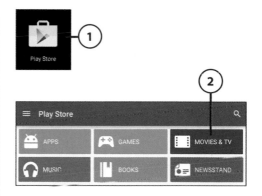

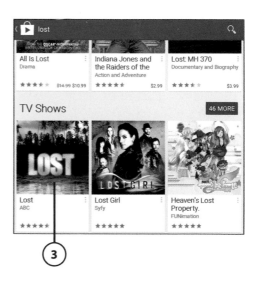

4. Tap to expand the synopsis.

5. Tap to add this TV series to your Wishlist.

6. Tap to change the season if the TV show has multiple seasons.

7. Tap to buy the entire season. When you buy a season that is not yet complete, as new episodes air on TV, you automatically have access to them on your tablet.

8. Tap to buy just one episode.

9. Tap to buy the Standard Definition (SD) version of the TV show season or episode. SD is lower quality.

10. Tap to buy the High Definition (HD) version of the TV show season or episode. HD is the best quality.

11. Tap Buy to complete your purchase.

Adding a Payment Method

Before you purchase TV shows, you need to make sure that you have a way to pay for it. To do that, you need to add a payment method to your Google Wallet account. To do this on your desktop computer, browse to http://wallet.google.com and log in. Click Payment Methods, and if you do not already have a valid payment method, click Add A Payment Method. Enter one of your valid debit or credit cards.

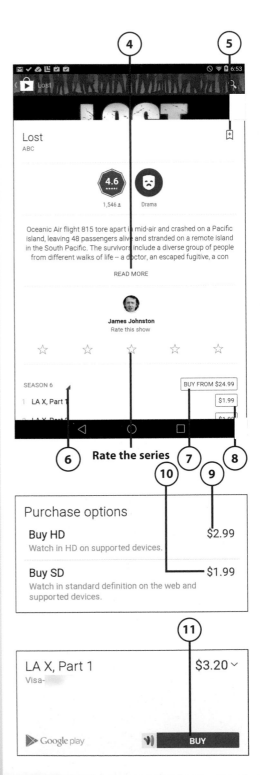

Use the Play Movies & TV App

When you watch movies and TV shows, they are actually playing inside an app called Play Movies & TV. You can launch this app when you want to watch movies and TV shows you have previously purchased or rented.

1. Tap to launch Play Movies & TV.

2. Tap to find more movies or TV shows in the Google Play store.

3. Scroll down to see movies and TV shows Google recommends for you based on what you have previously searched for, rented, or purchased.

4. Swipe in from the left of the screen to reveal the menu.

5. Tap My Library to see only movies you have purchased or rented, no matter if they are physically located on your tablet or still in the cloud.

6. Tap to see movies and TV shows that you have added to your Wishlist.

7. Tap to shop for more movies or TV shows in the Google Play store.

8. Tap to change the settings for the Play Movies & TV app. See the next section for an explanation of the settings.

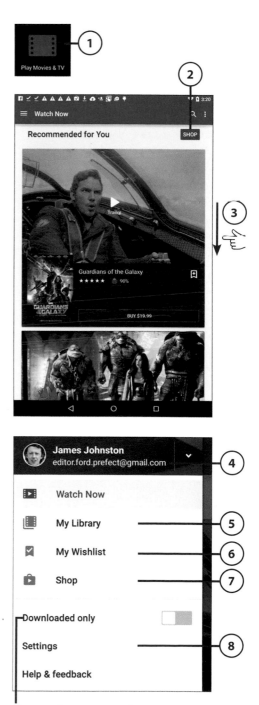

Show only movies and TV shows that have been downloaded to your tablet

Change Play Movies & TV Settings

1. Tap Show Cards on Pause to choose whether you want to see information about actors and songs featured at the current position in the movie or TV show you have paused.

2. Tap to choose to play back the original language from the movie or TV show, or try and force the playback of English audio when available.

3. Tap to enable or change the way Captions (Closed Captioning) looks systemwide (in this app and all other apps).

4. Tap to manage downloaded movies and TV shows. You can delete them to free up space, and view any downloads already in progress.

5. Tap Quality to choose whether to default to downloading High Definition (HD) content or Standard Definition (SD) content.

6. Tap to choose whether you want to hear 5.1 Surround Sound if the content you are playing supports it.

7. Tap to play a short demo of how 5.1 Surround Sound works.

8. Tap to save your changes and return to the Movies & TV main screen.

8

← Settings

General

Show cards on pause
Show information about the actors and songs featured at the current position in the video — **1**

Language and captions

Audio language
The video's original language — **2**

Caption settings
Set preferences for closed captions — **3**

Downloads

Manage downloads
Free up space and view downloads in progress — **4**

Quality
HD (Better quality) — **5**

Surround Sound

Enable surround sound
Activate surround sound, use 5.1 soundtrack when available — **6**

Play demo
Play a short demonstration of surround sound — **7**

Copy Videos from Your Computer

You can copy videos from your computer onto your Android tablet via the USB cable. You start by creating a folder on your tablet to store the videos and then you drag them from your computer to the new folder.

Windows

1. Connect your tablet to your PC using the supplied USB cable. It appears in Windows Explorer.

2. In Explorer, click the tablet. This example uses a Google Nexus 7.

3. Click Internal Storage to expand the list of folders on your tablet.

4. Right-click in the right pane.

5. Click New Folder.

6. Type a name for your new folder. The example folder is My Videos.

7. Click the newly created folder in the left pane.

8. Drag a movie from another folder on your PC to the new folder.

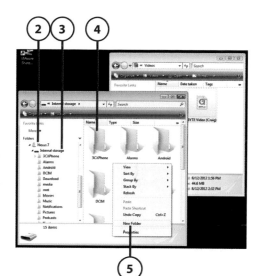

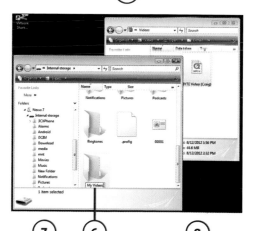

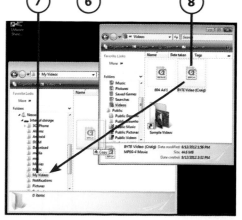

Apple Mac OSX

To copy files from your Mac to your tablet, you must install Android File Transfer. You should have done this already, but if not, please follow the instructions in the Prologue.

1. Connect your tablet to your Mac using the supplied USB cable. Android File Transfer automatically launches.

2. Click File.

3. Click New Folder.

4. Type a name for your new folder The example folder is My Videos.

5. Drag a movie from another folder on your Mac to the new folder.

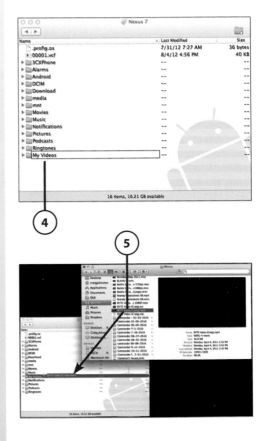

Watching Videos with YouTube

Your Android tablet comes with a YouTube app that enables you to find and watch videos, rate them, add them to your favorites, and share links to YouTube videos. The YouTube application even enables you to upload new videos.

Navigate the YouTube Main Screen

1. Tap the YouTube icon to launch the YouTube application.

2. Tap a video to open it.

3. Tap to search for a video on YouTube.

4. Tap to change the YouTube app settings.

5. Scroll down to see all videos in your What to Watch feed.

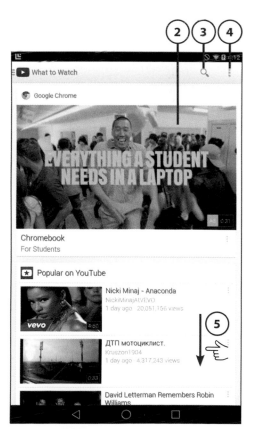

Navigate the YouTube App

1. Swipe in from the left of the screen to reveal a menu.

2. Tap My Subscriptions to see a mixture of videos from YouTube channels you subscribe to.

3. Tap to see videos you have uploaded to YouTube.

4. Tap to see your YouTube history including videos you have previously watched.

5. Tap to see a list of videos you have chosen to watch later. You find out how to set videos to be watched later in the next section.

6. Tap to see movies and TV shows you have previously purchased in the Google Play store. You can play that content in YouTube.

7. Tap one of your YouTube Playlists to see videos that have been added to it.

8. Tap one of the channels you subscribe to see videos in it.

9. Scroll down for more options.

10. Tap to browse YouTube channels.

11. Tap to see what is popular on YouTube.

12. Tap one of the Best of YouTube categories to see videos in them.

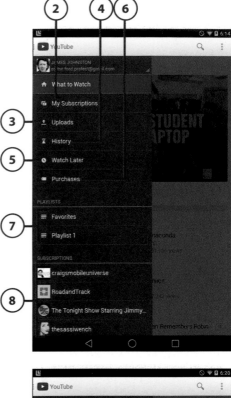

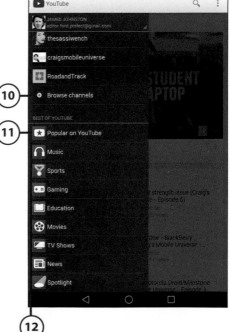

Play a Video

While playing a YouTube video, you can rate the video, read video comments, and share the video with someone.

1. Tap on the playing video to see options.

2. Tap to share a link to this video. You can share it on Facebook, Twitter, Google+, or by more traditional ways such as email and text message.

3. Tap to add this video to your favorites, save the video to an existing or new YouTube playlist, or add the video to your Watch Later queue.

4. Tap to give this video a thumbs up. Thumbs up tells the video's creator that you liked the video.

5. Tap to give this video a thumbs down. Thumbs down tells the video's creator that you disliked the video.

6. Scroll down to read and post comments for this video, but also see suggested videos. YouTube suggests videos that are related to the one you are watching based on content and keywords.

7. Tap to choose whether you want to show the Closed Captions (CC), play the Standard Definition (SD) or High Definition (HD) version of the video, or flag the video as innapropriate.

8. Tap to pause the video.

9. Tap to subscribe to the YouTube channel where this video is found.

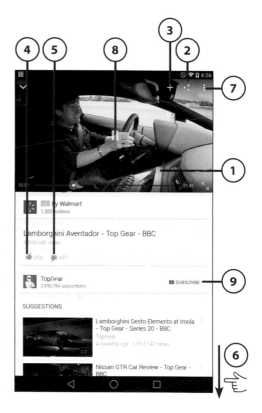

Viewing Videos Full Screen

To view a video at a larger size, simply rotate your Android tablet, and the video will be played in landscape mode.

Swipe Videos Away

While playing a video in a window (not full screen), if you swipe it down, it moves to the bottom right of the screen as a thumbnail. Swipe the thumbnail of the video up to make it large, or swipe it left to dismiss it.

Upload a Video

You can upload one of your personal videos to YouTube. When uploaded, you can share the video with others.

1. Swipe in from the left of the screen to reveal the menu.

2. Tap Uploads. You see videos that you have previously uploaded to YouTube.

3. Tap the upload icon.

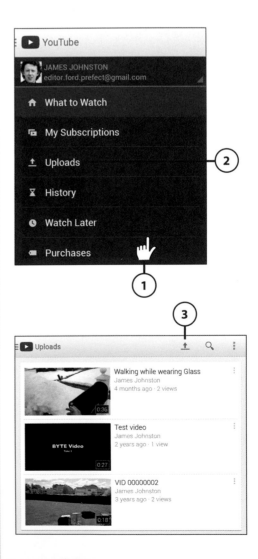

4. Select a video to upload from videos you have stored in the Photos app.

5. Tap to enter a title for your video.

6. Tap to enter a description for your video.

7. Tap to choose whether the video is private, public, or unlisted.

8. Tap to add any tags or keywords so that your video can be found if people search using the tags you enter.

9. Tap to upload your video.

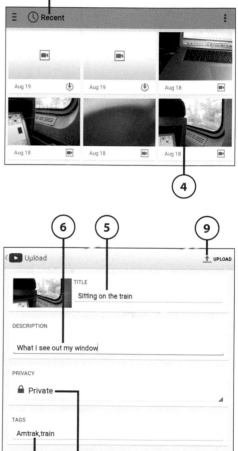

Tap to see other videos

Change YouTube Settings

If you want to clear your YouTube search history, set the video caption font size, or choose the SafeSearch Filter, you can do this in the YouTube application's settings screen.

1. Tap the Menu icon.

2. Tap Settings.

3. Tap General to choose whether to prioritize videos from a specific country, whether to send Google anonymous data about your YouTube usage, and whether you want to receive notifications about YouTube content.

4. Tap to manage connected TVs.

5. Tap Search to specify whether you want videos with restricted content to be hidden when you search, set YouTube to never remember your video viewing history, and to clear your YouTube history.

6. Tap to choose how Captions (Closed Captioning) look in the YouTube app.

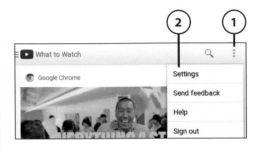

>>>Go Further
WHAT ARE CONNECTED TVS?

Smart TVs and game consoles that include the YouTube app can be used by your Android tablet's YouTube app as a second screen. After you pair a Smart TV or game console with your Android tablet, you can "send" a YouTube video to the TV or game console to be played. This enables you to let others watch the video with you.

Quickly control your
Bluetooth and Wi-Fi

This chapter covers your Android tablet's connectivity capabilities, including Bluetooth, Wi-Fi, VPN, and NFC. Topics include the following:

→ Pairing with Bluetooth devices

→ Connecting to Wi-Fi networks

→ Connecting to virtual private networks (VPNs)

→ Using Near Field Communications (NFC)

Connecting to Bluetooth, Wi-Fi, and VPNs

Your Android tablet can connect to Bluetooth devices—such as headsets, computers, and car in-dash systems—as well as to Wi-Fi networks. Your Android tablet can also connect to virtual private networks (VPNs) for access to secure networks and send information between your tablet and another Android device using Wi-Fi Direct.

Connecting to Bluetooth Devices

Bluetooth is a great personal area network (PAN) technology that enables short-distance wireless access to all sorts of devices, such as headsets, phones, and computers. The following tasks walk you through how to pair your Android tablet to your device and how to configure options.

Pair with a New Bluetooth Device

Before you can take advantage of Bluetooth, you need to connect your Android tablet with that device, which is called pairing. After you pair your Android tablet with a Bluetooth device, they can connect to each other automatically in the future.

First Put the Bluetooth Device into Pairing Mode

Before you pair a Bluetooth device to your Android tablet, you first must put the device into Pairing mode. If you pair with a Bluetooth headset, for example, the process normally involves holding the button on the headset for a certain period of time. Consult your Bluetooth device's manual to find out how to put that device into Pairing mode.

1. Pull down the Quick Settings Bar.

2. Tap the word Bluetooth to open the Bluetooth settings.

3. Tap the on switch to enable Bluetooth, if it is not already in the on position.

4. Tap the Bluetooth device you want to connect to. This example uses the Plantronics PLT_M165 headset.

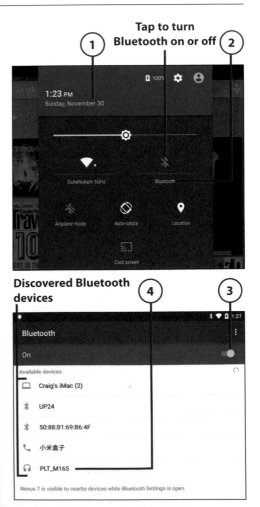

Tap to turn
1 **Bluetooth on or off** **2**

1:23 PM
Sunday, November 30

DukeNukem 5GHz   Bluetooth

Airplane mode   Auto-rotate   Location

Cast screen

Discovered Bluetooth **4**   **3**
devices

Bluetooth   ⋮

On

Available devices

☐ Craig's iMac (2)

⁎ UP24

⁎ 50:88:B1:69:B6:4F

☏ 小米盒子

🎧 PLT_M165

Nexus 7 is visible to nearby devices while Bluetooth Settings is open.

5. If all goes well, your Android tablet should now be paired with the new Bluetooth device.

Bluetooth

On

Paired devices

PLT_M165
Connected

Successfully paired

>>>Go Further
BLUETOOTH PASSKEY

If you pair with a device that requires a passkey, such as a computer, your car, or another smartphone or tablet, the screen shows a passkey. Make sure the passkey is the same on your Android tablet and on the device you are pairing with. Tap Pair on your Android tablet, and confirm the passkey on the device you are pairing with.

Bluetooth pairing request

Device
Craig's iMac (2)

Pairing code
339713

Pairing grants access to your contacts and call history when connected.

CANCEL   PAIR —— **Tap to confirm the passkey and pair**

If you pair with an older Bluetooth headset, you might be prompted to enter the passkey. Try using four zeroes as the passkey. It normally works. If the zeroes don't work, refer to the headset's manual.

Reverse Pairing

The steps in this section describe how to pair your Android tablet with a Bluetooth device that is in Pairing mode and listening for an incoming pairing command. You can pair Bluetooth another way by asking others to search for and pair with your tablet. Anytime you have the Bluetooth screen open, your tablet is in Pairing mode and listening for incoming pairing requests.

Extra Bluetooth Options

You can change the name your Android tablet uses when pairing over Bluetooth to make it easier to find, see any files people have sent you via Bluetooth, and re-scan for devices.

1. Tap the Menu icon.

2. Tap to refresh the list of discovered Bluetooth devices by re-scanning.

3. Tap to rename your Android tablet so that it has a friendlier name when seen over Bluetooth, Wi-Fi, and NFC.

4. Tap to see any files people have sent you via Bluetooth.

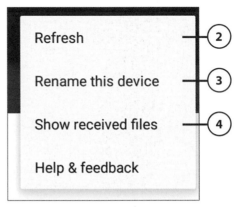

Change Bluetooth Device Options

After a Bluetooth device is paired, you can change a few options for some of them. The number of options depends on the Bluetooth device you connect to; some have more features than others.

1. Tap the Settings icon to the right of the Bluetooth device.

2. Tap to rename the Bluetooth device to something friendly.

3. Tap to disconnect and unpair from the Bluetooth device. If you do this, you can't use the device until you redo the pairing as described in the earlier task.

4. Tap to enable and disable what you want to use the Bluetooth device for. These features are called profiles; sometimes Bluetooth devices have more than one profile, as in this example.

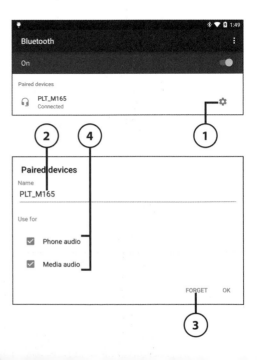

Bluetooth Profiles

Each Bluetooth device can have one or more Bluetooth profiles. Each Bluetooth profile describes certain features of the device. This tells your Android tablet what it can do when connected to it. A Bluetooth headset normally has only one profile, such as Phone Audio. This tells your Android tablet that it can use only the device for phone call audio. Some devices might have this profile but provide other features, such as a Phone Book Access profile, which would enable it to synchronize your Android tablet's address book, or Media Audio, which is for playing stereo music via Bluetooth. Read more about Bluetooth Profiles at http://en.wikipedia.org/wiki/List_of_Bluetooth_profiles.

Quick Disconnect

To quickly disconnect from a Bluetooth device, touch the device on the Bluetooth Settings screen, and then touch OK.

Wi-Fi

Wi-Fi (Wireless Fidelity) networks are wireless networks that run within free radio bands around the world. Your local coffee shop probably has free Wi-Fi, and so do many other public areas, such as airports, train stations, and malls. Your Android tablet can connect to any Wi-Fi network to provide you access to the Internet.

Connect to Wi-Fi

The following steps explain how to find and connect to Wi-Fi networks. After you connect your Android tablet to a Wi-Fi network, you are automatically connected to it the next time you are in range of that network.

1. Pull down the Quick Settings Bar.

2. Tap the word Wi-Fi to go to the Wi-Fi settings.

3. Tap to turn Wi-Fi on if the slider is in the off position.

4. Tap the name of the Wi-Fi network you want to connect to. If the network does not use any security, you can skip to Step 7.

5. Enter the Wi-Fi network password.

6. Tap to show advanced options if you need to specify a Proxy or change the way that your IP address is assigned.

7. Tap to connect to the Wi-Fi network.

Adding a Hidden Network

If the network you want to connect to is not listed on the screen, it might be purposely hidden. If it is hidden, it does not broadcast its name, which is also known as its Service Set Identifier (SSID). Tap the Menu icon, and tap Add Network. Type in the SSID, and choose the type of security that the network uses. You need to get this information from the network administrator before you try connecting.

8. If all goes well, you see the Wi-Fi network in the list with the word Connected under it.

Can't Connect to Wi-Fi?

If all does not go well, you might be typing the password or encryption key incorrectly. Verify both with the person who owns the Wi-Fi network. It might be easier to make use of Wi-Fi Protected Setup (WPS) if it is available. WPS still allows for a secure connection, but it removes the need to type long network passwords.

Indicates Wi-Fi signal strength

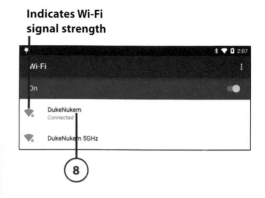

Connecting to Wi-Fi Protected Setup (WPS) Networks

Many new Wi-Fi routers include a method of connecting called Wi-Fi Protected Setup (WPS). The idea is that on the Wi-Fi router, you press a button to start the WPS connection. On your tablet, you touch the WPS icon, and the two devices automatically connect to each other in a secure way. Sometimes, a WPS-enabled router uses a method in which you swap PINs. Your tablet supports both methods of connecting via WPS. Tap the Menu icon, then tap Advanced, and choose the method of WPS you want to use.

Wi-Fi Direct

WPS Push Button ———————————— **Tap to use the WPS push-button method**

Tap to use the ——WPS Pin Entry
WPS PIN method

Adjust Wi-Fi Network Options

1. Tap a Wi-Fi network to reveal a pop-up that shows information about your connection to that network.

2. Tap Forget to tell your Android tablet to not connect to this network in the future.

3. Touch and hold on a Wi-Fi network to reveal two actions.

4. Tap to forget the Wi-Fi network and no longer connect to it.

5. Tap to change the Wi-Fi network password that your Android tablet uses to connect to the network, or modify other settings for this network.

6. Tap to write the information about this Wi-Fi network onto an NFC tag, allowing others to simply scan the tag to connect. You need to have the NFC radio turned on and an NFC tag in range.

Set Advanced Wi-Fi Options

You can configure a few advanced Wi-Fi settings that can help preserve the battery life of your Android tablet.

1. Tap the Menu icon.

2. Tap Advanced.

3. Tap to enable or disable the capability for your Android tablet to automatically notify you when it detects a new Wi-Fi network.

4. Tap to enable or disable the capability for Google's location service and other apps to scan for Wi-Fi networks, even if you have turned off Wi-Fi.

5. Tap to change the Wi-Fi sleep policy. This enables you to choose if your Android tablet should keep its connection to Wi-Fi when the tablet goes to sleep.

6. Tap to manually set the frequency bands that your tablet uses when communicating over Wi-Fi. You can choose 2.4 GHz or 5 GHz. It is better to leave this set to Auto to allow your tablet to automatically select the best option.

7. Tap to install certificates used to secure Wi-Fi communications. Your company's IT admin may email you a certificate to install before you connect to your company's Wi-Fi network.

8. Tap to manage Wi-Fi Direct connections.

9. Tap to connect using WPS Push Button or WPS Pin Entry.

10. Use this Wi-Fi MAC address if you need to provide a network administrator with your MAC address to use a Wi-Fi network.

11. This shows the IP address assigned to your Android tablet when it connected to the Wi-Fi network.

12. Tap to save your changes and return to the previous screen.

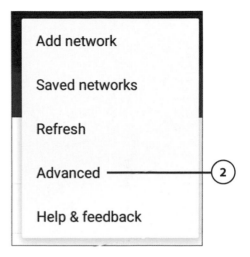

Should You Keep Wi-Fi on During Sleep?

In Step 5 you can choose how your Android tablet handles its connection to Wi-Fi when it goes to sleep. If your tablet has no cellular data, Wi-Fi is the only way that it can connect to the Internet. You should keep this option set to Always; otherwise, any real-time updates cannot be delivered to you, and your tablet cannot update things such as email. However, battery usage can be affected by always maintaining a Wi-Fi connection, and you might want to set this to Only When Plugged In, which means that if your Android tablet is not charging, and it goes to sleep, it turns Wi-Fi off. When the tablet is charging and it goes to sleep, it stays connected to Wi-Fi. If you set this setting to Never, it means that when your Android tablet goes to sleep, it turns Wi-Fi off.

>>>Go Further

WHAT ARE IP AND MAC ADDRESSES?

A MAC address is a number burned into your Android tablet that identifies its Wi-Fi adapter. This is called the physical layer because it is a physical adapter. An IP address is a secondary way to identify your Android tablet. Unlike a MAC address, the IP address can be changed anytime. Modern networks use the IP address when they need to deliver some data to you. Typically, when you connect to a network, a device on the network assigns you a new IP address. On home networks, this device is typically your Wi-Fi router.

Some network administrators use a security feature to limit who can connect to their Wi-Fi networks. They set up their networks to allow connections from only Wi-Fi devices with specific MAC addresses. If you try to connect to such a network, you have to give the network administrator your MAC address so that he can add it to the allowed list.

Virtual Private Networks (VPNs)

Your Android tablet can connect to virtual private networks (VPNs), which are normally used by companies to provide a secure connection to their inside networks or intranets.

Add a VPN

Before you add a VPN, you must first have all the information needed to set it up on your Android tablet. Speak to your network administrator and get this information ahead of time to save frustration. This information includes the type of VPN protocol used, the type of encryption used, and the name of the host to which you are connecting.

1. Pull down the Quick Settings Bar and tap the Settings icon.

2. Tap More under the Wireless & Networks section.

3. Tap VPN.

4. Tap OK to set up a lock screen PIN. If you already have a lock screen lock or password, you won't be prompted at this point, and you can proceed to Step 8.

Why Do You Need to Set a PIN?

If you don't already have a lock screen PIN, password, or pattern set up before you create your first VPN network connection, you are prompted to create one. This is a security measure that ensures your Android tablet must first be unlocked before anyone can access a stored VPN connection. Because VPN connections are usually used to access company data, this is a good idea.

5. Choose either Pattern, PIN, or Password to unlock your Android tablet.

6. Enter your lock screen PIN, pattern, or password. After you make your entry, you will be taken back to the main VPN screen.

7. Tap the plus icon to add a VPN profile.

8. Enter a name for your VPN network. You can call it anything such as **Work VPN** or the name of the provider such as **PublicVPN**.

9. Tap to choose the type of security the VPN network uses. Based on what you choose here, the additional information you need to enter in Step 10 will vary.

10. Enter the remaining parameters that your network administrator has provided.

11. Tap Save.

← VPN   🔍 + ⋮

Edit VPN profile

Name
Public VPN

Type
L2TP/IPSec PSK   ▼

Server address
gateway.publicvpn.net

L2TP secret
(not used)

IPSec identifier
(not used)

IPSec pre-shared key
•••••••••

DNS search domains
(not used)

DNS servers (e.g. 8.8.8.8)
(not used)

Forwarding routes (e.g. 10.0.0.0/8)
(not used)

                                    CANCEL   SAVE

Connect to a VPN

After you create one or more VPN connections, you can connect to them when you want to.

1. Pull down the Quick Settings Bar, and tap the Settings icon.

2. Tap More under the Wireless & Networks section.

🔋 100% ⚙ 👤

6:47 AM
Monday, December 1

Settings   🔍

Wireless & networks

📶 Wi-Fi   ✳ Bluetooth

🔄 Data usage   ••• More

3. Tap VPN.

4. Tap a preconfigured VPN connection.

5. Enter the VPN username.

6. Enter the VPN password.

7. Tap Connect. After you connect to the VPN, you can use your Android tablet's web browser and other applications normally, but you now have access to resources at the other end of the VPN tunnel, such as company web servers or even your company email.

← More

Airplane mode

NFC
Allow data exchange when the tablet touches another device

Android Beam
Ready to transmit app content via NFC

Tethering & portable hotspot

VPN

← VPN

Public VPN
L2TP/IPSec VPN with pre-shared keys

Connect to Public VPN

Username
fprefect

Password
••••••••••

☑ Save account information

CANCEL   CONNECT

**Check to save username
and password**

How Can You Tell If You Are Connected?

After your Android tablet successfully connects to a VPN network, you see a key icon in the Notification Bar. This indicates that you are connected. If you pull down the Notification Bar, you can tap the icon to see information about the connection and to disconnect from the VPN.

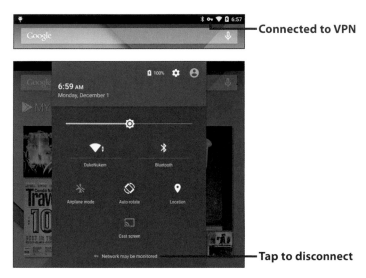

Connected to VPN

Tap to disconnect

Edit or Delete a VPN

You can edit an existing VPN or delete it by tapping and holding on the name of the VPN. A window pops up with a list of options.

>>>*Go Further*

ACCESS YOUR VPN QUICKLY

As you can see from the preceding task, it takes three steps to get to the VPN Settings screen. If you use a VPN connection often and want to minimize the steps, you can create a shortcut on your Home screen that takes you straight to the VPN settings screen. To do this, you need to find the Settings Shortcut Widget. Tap and hold it. and then drag it to the Home screen where you want it to stay. When you release the widget, you see a list of settings screens. Scroll down to VPN and tap it. Learn more about Home screen widgets in Chapter 9, "Customizing Your Android Tablet."

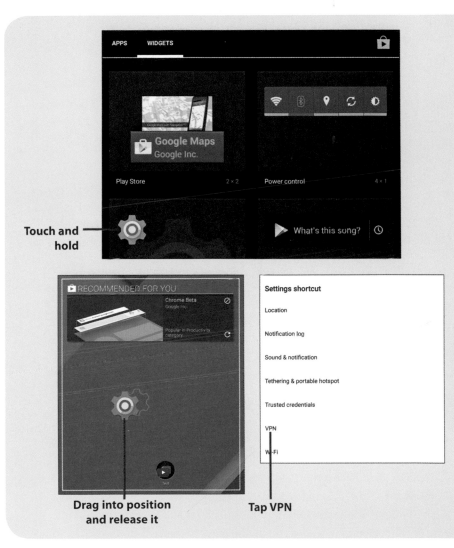

Touch and hold

Drag into position and release it

Tap VPN

>>>*Go Further*

ALWAYS-ON VPN

Some companies require you to use an Always-on VPN. Your Android tablet supports these kinds of VPNs. To use an Always-on VPN, first set up the VPN connection as detailed in this section. While on the VPN screen, tap the Menu icon, and
tap Always-on VPN. Finally, choose which previously configured VPN connection
you want to be Always-on.

Near Field Communications (NFC)

Your Android tablet has the capability to swap data via its Near Field Communications (NFC) radio with other devices that use NFC or read data that
is stored on NFC tags. You can also use NFC to pay for items you have purchased using Google Wallet. Here is how to start using NFC.

>>>*Go Further*

WHAT IS NFC?

NFC stands for Near Field Communications, a standard that enables devices such
as mobile phones or tablets to swap information or simply read information.
Think of NFC as a much lower-power version of Radio Frequency Identification
(RFID), which has been used for decades in applications such as electronic toll
(etoll) payments (when you drive through toll plazas and have the money automatically deducted from your account). The only difference is that with NFC you
must bring the two devices within about an inch of each other before they can
communicate.

Your Android tablet has an NFC radio, which you can use to read NFC tags,
swap information between two NFC-enabled devices (such as two NFC-enabled
phones or tablets), and send information to another phone or device. As more
phones start shipping with NFC built in, this technology will become more
useful.

Enable NFC

NFC is enabled by default but just in case you have disabled it, here is how to re-enable it.

1. Pull down the Quick Settings Bar and tap the Settings icon.

2. Tap More.

3. Tap to flip the switch to the on position to enable NFC data exchange.

App no longer
used for email

Tap to work with
your email

In this chapter, you learn about your Android tablet's email application, Gmail, and how to use it for not only your Gmail account, but also for other personal accounts using POP3, IMAP, and even your work email using Exchange. Topics include the following:

→ Sending and receiving email
→ Working with attachments
→ Working with Gmail labels
→ Changing settings

Email

Your Android tablet comes with an email app called Gmail. This app works with Google's free email service called Gmail, but it also supports other email services provided by other companies that support the POP3 and IMAP post office protocols, and even corporate email systems such as Microsoft Exchange and Lotus Notes.

What About the Email App?

In previous versions of Android, you would use the Email app for Exchange, POP3, and IMAP, and use the Gmail app for Gmail only. Now the Gmail app does it all. If you tap on the Email app, you see a message telling you to use Gmail.

Adding Accounts To Gmail

When you first set up your Android tablet, you set up, or log in, to a Google account that comes with a Gmail account. The Gmail application enables you to have multiple Gmail accounts, which is useful if you have a business account and a personal account. In this section we will set up an additional Gmail account, a POP3/IMAP account, and an Exchange account for work emails.

1. Tap to open the Gmail app.

2. Swipe in from the left of the screen to reveal the Gmail folders and the menu.

3. Tap Settings near the bottom of the menu. (Swipe down past the folders to see the Settings menu item if needed.)

4. Tap Add Account.

5. Follow the steps in the next few sections to add a Google account, personal account, and work account.

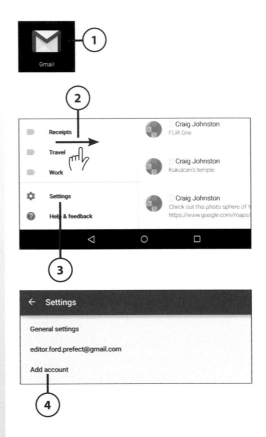

Add a Google Account

When you first set up your Android tablet, you added your first Google (Gmail) account. The following steps describe how to add a second account.

1. Tap Google.

2. Tap OK.

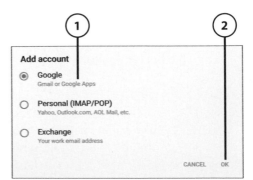

3. Enter your existing Google account name. This is your Gmail address.

4. Tap Next.

What If I Don't Have a Second Google Account?

If you don't already have a second Google account but want to set one up, in Step 3, tap Create a New Account. Your Android tablet walks you through the steps of setting up a new Google account.

5. Enter your existing Google password.

6. Tap Next.

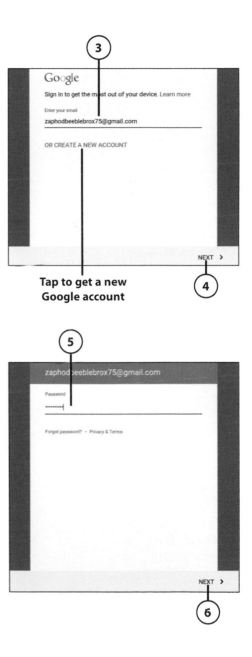

Tap to get a new
Google account

7. Select what components of your Google account you want to synchronize with your Android tablet. Scroll up and down to see all components.

8. Tap Next.

Why Multiple Google Accounts?

You are probably wondering why you would want multiple Google accounts. Isn't one good enough? Actually it is not that uncommon to have multiple Google accounts. It can be a way to compartmentalize your life between work and play. You might run a small business using the one account, but email only friends with another. Your Android tablet supports multiple accounts but still enables you to interact with them in one place.

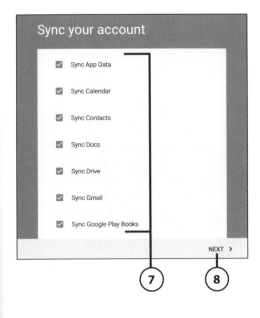

Add a New POP3 or IMAP Account

You can skip to the next section if you don't want to add a POP or IMAP email account. Email accounts from your Internet service provider or personal website probably use either POP3 or IMAP.

1. Tap Personal (IMAP/POP).

2. Tap OK.

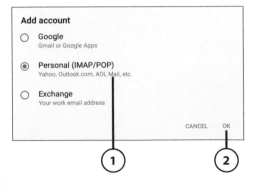

3. Enter the email address for this account.

4. Tap Next.

Why Manual Setup?

Your Android tablet tries to figure out the settings to set up your email account. This works most of the time when you use common email providers such as Yahoo! or Hotmail. It also works with large ISPs such as Comcast, Road Runner, Optimum Online, and so on. It might not work for smaller ISPs, in smaller countries, or when you create your own website and set up your own email. In these cases, you need to set up your email manually.

5. Tap either POP3 or IMAP as the type of account. If your email provider supports it, always choose IMAP. In this example, we choose IMAP.

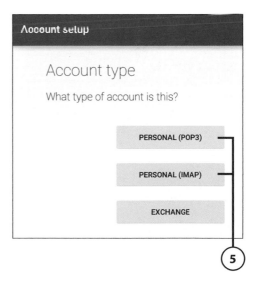

6. Enter the password for this email account, and then tap Next.

7. Ensure that the information on this screen for the incoming mail server is accurate. Pay close attention to the Server and Security Type fields as they may not be correct. Change them if needed.

8. Tap Next.

Where Can I Find This Information?

Always check your ISP's or email service provider's website and look for instructions on how to set up your email on a computer or smartphone. This is normally under the support section of the website.

Username and Password

On the Incoming Server and Outgoing Server screens, your username and password should already be filled out because you typed them in earlier. If not, enter them. Typically for POP3 and IMAP setups, the username is your full email address.

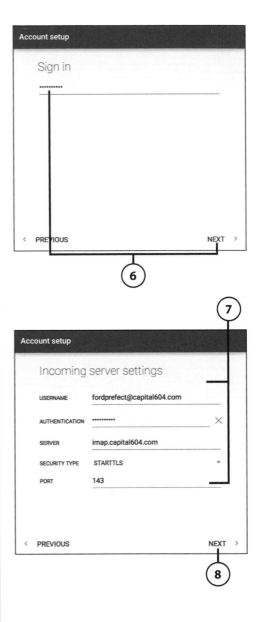

9. Ensure that the information on this screen for the outgoing mail server is accurate. Pay close attention to the Server and Security Type fields, as they may not be correct. Change them if needed.

10. Tap Next.

11. Tap to change the frequency in which email from this account synchronizes to your Android tablet, or set it to Never to only get new mail when you open the Gmail app.

12. Check the box if you want to be notified when new email arrives into this account.

13. Check the box if you want email to synchronize between this account and your Android tablet.

14. Check the box if you want email to be automatically downloaded when you are connected to a Wi-Fi network. Tap the right arrow at the bottom of the screen when you're done with the options on this page.

15. Enter a friendly name for this account, such as **Capital 604 Mail**.

16. Enter your full name or the name you want to display when people receive emails sent from this account.

17. Tap Next.

Be Secure if You Can

If your mail provider supports email security such as SSL or TLS, you should strongly consider using it. If you don't, emails you send and receive go over the Internet in plain readable text. Using SSL or TLS encrypts the emails as they travel across the Internet so that nobody can read them. Set this under the Advanced settings for the Incoming and Outgoing Servers.

Account setup

Outgoing server settings

SMTP SERVER	smtp.capital604.com
SECURITY TYPE	STARTTLS
PORT	587

☑ Require signin

USERNAME	fordprefect@capital604.com
AUTHENTICATION	....

< PREVIOUS   NEXT >

Account setup

Account options

Sync frequency: Every 15 minutes

☑ Notify me when email arrives

☑ Sync email from this account

☑ Automatically download attachments when connected to Wi-Fi

Account setup

Your account is set up and email is on its way!

Give this account a name (optional)
Capital 604 Mail

Your name (displayed on outgoing messages)
Ford Prefect

NEXT >

Add a Work Email Account

You can skip to the next section if you don't want to add a work email account. Work email systems must support Microsoft Exchange to work on your tablet.

1. Tap Exchange.

2. Tap OK.

3. Enter your company email address.

4. Tap Next.

5. Type the password for your work email account.

6. Tap Next.

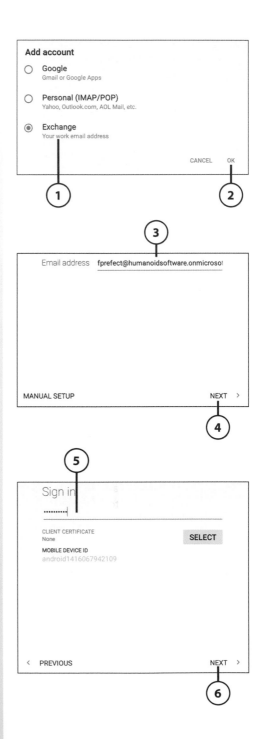

Add account

○ Google
Gmail or Google Apps

○ Personal (IMAP/POP)
Yahoo, Outlook.com, AOL Mail, etc.

◉ Exchange
Your work email address

CANCEL   OK

①   **②**

③

Email address   fprefect@humanoidsoftware.onmicrosof

MANUAL SETUP   NEXT ›

④

⑤

Sign in

•••••••••

CLIENT CERTIFICATE
None   SELECT

MOBILE DEVICE ID
android1416067942109

‹ PREVIOUS   NEXT ›

⑥

7. Check the username and change it if necessary. Many times the username is not your email address but rather the username you use to login to your company's network.

8. Enter the email server.

9. Tap Next.

10. Tap OK to allow the company's email server to remotely control your tablet. The extent to which they control it differs by company.

11. Tap to choose to either have your email pushed to your tablet in real-time as it arrives in your company Inbox, or on a schedule.

12. Tap to choose how many days in the past email is synchronized to your Android tablet, or set it to All to synchronize all email in your Inbox.

13. Tap to enable or disable being notified when new email arrives from your corporate Inbox.

14. Tap to enable or disable synchronizing your corporate contacts to your Android tablet.

15. Tap to enable or disable synchronizing your corporate calendar to your Android tablet.

16. Tap to enable or disable synchronizing your corporate email to your Android tablet.

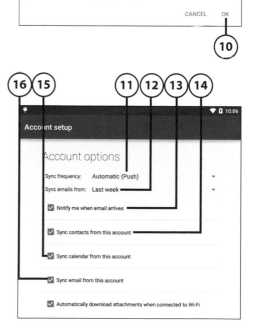

17. Tap to enable or disable automatically downloading email attachments when your Android tablet is connected to a Wi-Fi network.

What to Synchronize

You might decide that you don't want to synchronize all your work information to your Android tablet. You might decide to just synchronize email but not the calendar, or maybe just the calendar but not the contacts and email. Unchecking these boxes enables you to choose the information you don't want to synchronize. You can go back into the account settings and change it later if you change your mind.

18. Tap the Next icon.

19. Tap Activate to allow your company's email server to add restrictions on your tablet. The message displayed on the screen is a standard message indicating what your company can do, but is not representative of what they will do.

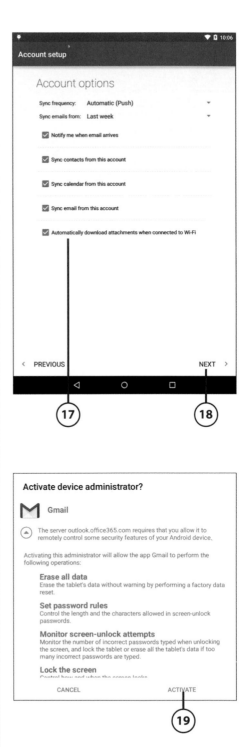

20. Enter a friendly name for your work email account, if you want to.

21. Tap Next to complete your company email setup.

Navigate the Gmail App

Let's take a quick look at the Gmail app and find out how to navigate the main screen.

1. Tap the Gmail icon to launch the app. Your initial view will be of the Inbox of your primary Google (Gmail) account, which is the account you used when setting up your tablet.

2. Tap to search the current folder for an email.

3. Tap to compose a new email.

4. Tap to see only new messages received from your social networking sites such as Facebook and Google+. When you have tapped it once, the Social option disappears until new social media emails arrive.

5. Tap to see any new emails that are promotions for products. When you have tapped it once, the Promotions option disappears until more promotional emails arrive.

6. Tap to see any new updates. Updates include messages about updating an app, but can also include email relating to things you have purchased, bills you need to pay, and even updates to meeting invites. After you have tapped Updates once, the Updates option disappears until there are more new updates.

7. Tap to access Social, Promotions, and Updates anytime.

8. Tap to see messages from any forums you are participating in.

9. Tap your other email accounts to switch to them, if you have more than one.

10. Swipe the vertical action bar to the right to expand it.

11. Tap to switch between your email accounts, if you have more than one.

12. Tap to add a new email account.

13. Tap to manage your existing email accounts.

14. Tap the current email account to see a list of folders (or as the Gmail app calls them, Labels).

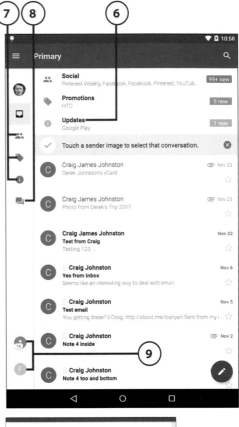

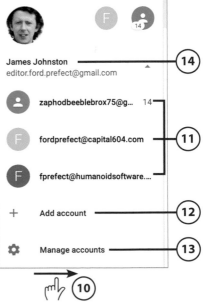

15. Tap to view Social, Promotions, Updates, and Forums. These are only visible when viewing Google (Gmail) accounts.

16. Tap to switch between your different folders, or as the Gmail app calls them, labels.

17. Scroll down to see all your labels.

18. Swipe the vertical action bar to the left to minimize it.

Stars and Labels

In the Gmail app, you use stars and labels to help organize your email. In most email clients you can create folders in your mailbox to help you organize your emails. For example, you might create a folder called "emails from the boss" and move any emails you receive from your boss to that folder. The Gmail app doesn't use the term folders; it uses the term labels instead. You can create labels in Gmail and choose an email to label. When you label the email, it actually moves it to a folder with that label. Any email that you mark with a star is actually just getting a label called "starred." But when viewing your Gmail, you see the yellow star next to an email. People normally add a star to an email as a reminder of something important.

Compose an Email

1. Tap the compose icon.

2. Tap to change the email account from which the message is being sent (if you have multiple accounts).

3. Type names in the To field. If the name matches someone in your Contacts, a list of choices is displayed and you can tap a name to select it. If you only know the email address, type it here.

4. Tap to add Carbon Copy (CC) or Blind Carbon Copy (BCC) recipients.

5. Tap the paperclip icon to add one or more attachments or to insert links to one or more Google Drive files.

6. Type a subject for your email.

7. Type the body of the email.

8. Tap to save the email as a draft, or discard it.

9. Tap to send the email.

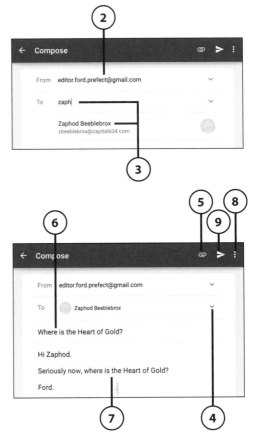

Add Attachments or Insert Drive Links

Before sending an email, you can add one or more attachments or insert links to files you have in your Google Drive account. The Gmail app can attach files found on your tablet and in your Google Drive account. Here is how to add attachments and link Drive documents.

1. After filling in the fields as described in the "Compose an Email" task, tap the paperclip icon.

2. Tap either Attach File or Insert from Drive. In this example, we tap Attach File.

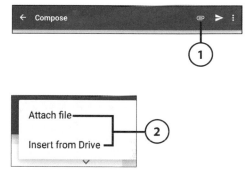

What Is The Difference Between Attaching and Inserting?

When you choose to attach a file to an email, you can choose a file located on your tablet, in the Photos app, or in your Google Drive account. The file is then copied from that location and attached to the email. If you choose to insert a file from Google Drive, then the file you choose is not actually copied out of Google Drive and attached to the email, but rather a link to that file is placed in the body of the email. This allows the recipients to tap the link and open the document right in your Google Drive account.

3. Choose where you want to search for the file. This can include your recent downloads, your Google Drive account, the Downloads folder, internal tablet storage, or the Photos app.

4. Tap the file to attach it. In this example the attachment is a document in my Google Drive account.

5. Tap Send.

6. If you inserted files from Google Drive, you need to choose what privileges recipients have. Tap to choose whether recipients can simply view the files, comment on them, or edit them.

7. Tap Send.

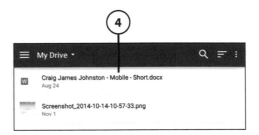

Links to Drive files

Attachments

Tap the X to remove an attachment

Force recipients to request access

Read an Email

1. Tap an email to open it. Unread emails are in bold and emails you have already read are not bold.

2. Tap to mark the email as unread and return to the email list view.

Rich Text Formatting

Rich Text Formatting (RTF) is a message formatted with anything that is not plain text. RTF includes bulleted lists, different fonts, font colors, font sizes, and styles such as bold, italic, and underline. Although you cannot type an email on your tablet with the standard keyboard using RTF, if you are sent an RTF email, your tablet preserves the formatting and displays it correctly.

3. Tap to reply to the sender of the email. This does not reply to anyone in the CC field.

4. Tap the Menu icon to reply to the sender of the email and any recipients in the To and CC fields (Reply All). You can also choose to print the email.

5. Tap to forward the email to someone.

What Are Conversations?

Conversations are Gmail's version of email threads. When you look at the main view of the Gmail app, you are seeing a list of email conversations. The conversation might have only one email in it, but to Gmail that's a conversation. As you and others reply to that original email, Gmail groups those emails in a thread, or conversation.

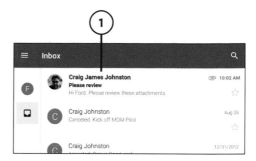

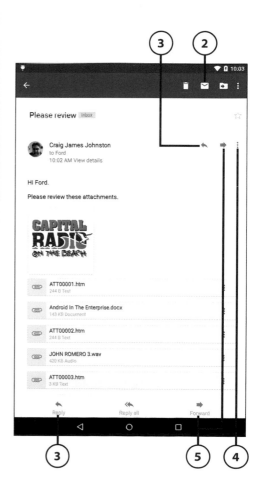

6. Tap to expand the email header to see all recipients and all other email header information.

7. Tap to "star" the message, or move it to the "starred" label.

8. Tap the sender's contact picture to see more contact information about him.

9. Tap to reply to the email and all recipients (Reply All).

10. Tap to move the email to the Trash folder.

11. Tap to move the email to a different label.

12. Tap attachments to open them.

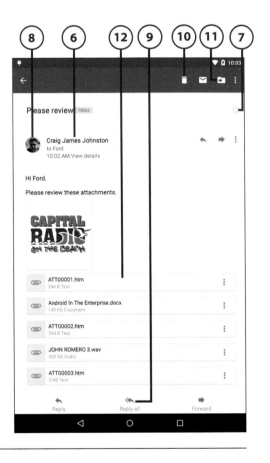

Gmails Have Extra Options

If you are receiving email in your Gmail Inbox, you will have a few extra options while reading an email that are specific to Gmail. You can Archive an email as well as send it to Trash. You can also mark an email as important, mute the email conversation, report an email as spam, or report an email as a phishing scam. When you mute a conversation, you will no longer see any emails in that conversation (or email thread). For more information on printing emails, and an explanation on what an important email is, see the notes that follow.

>>>*Go Further*

HOW DO I PRINT EMAILS?

When you choose to print an email, the print dialog enables you to choose to print the email to a PDF (which turns the email into a Portable Document Format [PDF] file) or to print the email to any printers that you have previously connected to Google Cloud Print using your desktop Chrome web browser. To learn more about how to connect your printers to your Google Cloud Print account, look at the instructions at https://support.google.com/chrome/answer/1069693?hl=en.

Tap to choose a printer or save as a PDF

What Is Important?

Gmail tries to automatically figure out which of the emails you receive are important. As it learns, it might sometimes be wrong. If an email is marked as important but it is not important, you can manually change the status to not important. Important emails have a yellow arrow whereas emails that are not important have a clear arrow. All emails marked as Important are also given the Priority Inbox label.

What Happens to Your Spam or Phishing Emails?

When you mark an email in Gmail as spam or as a phishing scam, two things happen. First, it gets a label called Spam. Second, a copy of that email is sent to Gmail's spam servers so that they are now aware of a possible new spam email that is circulating around the Internet. Based on what the servers see for all Gmail users, they block the emails that have been marked as spam and phishing emails from reaching other Gmail users. So the bottom line is that you should always mark spam emails because it helps all of us.

Customize Gmail App Settings

You can customize the way the Gmail app works, as well as how each independent email account functions.

1. Swipe in from the left of the screen and tap on the current email account to reveal its folders.

2. Tap Settings.

3. Tap General Settings.

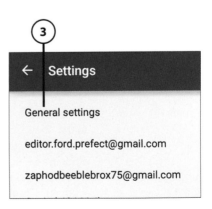

4. Tap to choose what must be shown when you choose to archive or delete a message. The choices are Archive or Delete.

5. Check the box to enable the ability to swipe an email left or right to archive it.

6. Check the box to enable showing the email sender's contact image in the conversation list.

7. Check the box to enable making Reply All as the default reply action.

8. Tap to enable automatically shrinking the emails to fit on the screen.

9. Tap to choose what happens when you archive or delete a message. Your choices are to show newer messages, older messages, or the conversation list.

10. Choose which actions you want to show a confirmation screen for.

11. Tap to save your changes and return to the main Settings screen.

12. Tap one of your accounts to change settings specific to that account, and follow the steps in the sections that follow.

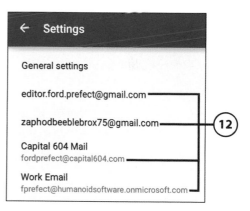

Additional Options in General Settings

While in the General Settings screen, if you tap the Menu icon, you can clear your email search history, or clear picture approvals. When you clear picture approvals, you are clearing your previous decisions on which emails you wanted to automatically load the images for.

Customize Google Account Settings

1. Tap to choose whether you want to see your Priority Inbox instead of your regular Inbox when opening the Gmail app.

What Is the Priority Inbox?

Google introduced the Priority Inbox as a way to automatically figure out which emails are important to you and place them in a folder called Priority Inbox. It does this by analyzing which emails you open and reply to. If it makes a mistake, you can mark a message as less important or more important. Over time, Google's handle on which emails are important to you gets more accurate. Because the Priority Inbox probably has the most-important emails, you might want to open it first and then go to the regular Inbox later to handle less-important emails. Read more about the Priority Inbox at http://mail.google.com/mail/help/priority-inbox.html.

2. Tap to choose what Inbox categories will be shown. As shown earlier in the chapter, by default the Social and Promotions categories are displayed. You can also show Updates and Forums.

3. Tap to enable or disable notifications when new email arrives for this Gmail account.

4. Tap to select how to get notified when new email arrives for this account. You can choose a different notification for each label and also decide which labels in addition to the Primary label you will be notified for.

5. Tap to enter a signature to be included at the end of all emails composed using this account.

6. Tap to set your Vacation Responder. This is a message that is automatically sent to people when you are on vacation.

7. Tap to choose whether to synchronize Gmail to this tablet. Turning this off stops Gmail from arriving on your tablet.

8. Tap to choose how many days of email to synchronize to your tablet.

9. Touch to manage labels. Labels are like folders. You can choose which labels synchronize to your tablet, how much email synchronizes, and what ringtone to play when new email arrives in that label.

10. Check the box to automatically download attachments to recently received emails while connected to a Wi-Fi network.

11. Tap to choose how images embedded in emails are handled. They can be automatically downloaded, or you can be prompted before they are downloaded for each email.

12. Tap to save your changes and return to the main Settings screen.

editor.ford.prefect@gmail.com

Inbox type
Default Inbox

Inbox categories
Primary, Social, Promotions, Updates, Forums

Notifications

Inbox sound
Sound on, notify once

Signature
Not set

Vacation responder
Off

Data usage

Sync Gmail

Days of mail to sync
30 days

Manage labels

Download attachments
Auto-download attachments to recent messages via Wi-Fi

Images
Always show

Email Signature

An email signature is a bit of text that is automatically added to the bottom of any email you send from your Android tablet. It is added when you compose a new email, reply to an email, or forward an email. A typical use for a signature is to automatically add your name and maybe some contact information at the end of your emails. Email signatures are sometimes referred to as email footers.

Customize POP/IMAP Account Settings

1. Tap to change the name of your account. This is the friendly name you may have typed when you originally set it up on your tablet.

2. Tap to change the full name you want people to see when you reply to emails using this account.

3. Tap to enter a signature to be included at the end of all emails composed using this account.

4. Tap to change the frequency in which your tablet checks for new email for this account. You can set it to Never, which means that your tablet will only check for email when you open the Gmail app, or you can set it to automatically check between every 15 minutes to every hour.

5. Check the box to automatically download attachments to recently received emails while connected to a Wi-Fi network.

6. Tap to enable or disable notifications when new email arrives for this email account.

7. Tap to select the ringtone to play when you are notified of new email for this account.

8. Tap to change the incoming email server settings for this account.

9. Tap to change the outgoing email server settings for this account.

10. Tap to save your changes and return to the main Settings screen.

Customize Exchange Account Settings

1. Tap to change the name of your account. This is the friendly name you may have typed when you originally set it up on your tablet.

2. Tap to change the full name you want people to see when you reply to emails using this account.

3. Tap to enter a signature to be included at the end of all emails composed using this account.

4. Tap to change the frequency in which your tablet checks for new email for this account. You can set it to Automatic (Push) to have emails automatically pushed to your tablet as soon as they arrive in your Inbox back at the office. You can also set it to Never, which means that your tablet will only check for email when you open the Gmail app, or you can set it to automatically check between every 15 minutes to every hour.

5. Tap to choose how much email to synchronize to your tablet. You can choose All to have every email synchronize, or choose between the last day up to the last month.

6. Tap to choose which folders to synchronize to your tablet. You will see a list of all mail folders, and you can choose whether to synchronize it or not, plus decide how much email should synchronize on a folder by folder basis.

7. Check the box to synchronize email from this account with your tablet. If you uncheck this box, email will stop synchronizing to your tablet.

8. Check the box to synchronize contacts from this account with your tablet. If you uncheck this box, contacts will stop synchronizing to your tablet.

9. Check the box to synchronize the calendar from this account with your tablet. If you uncheck this box, the calendar will stop synchronizing to your tablet.

10. Check the box to automatically download attachments to recently received emails while connected to a Wi-Fi network.

11. Scroll own for notification settings.

12. Tap to enable or disable notifications when new email arrives for this email account.

13. Tap to select the ringtone to play when you are notified of new email for this account.

14. Tap to change the incoming email server settings for this account.

15. Tap to save your changes and return to the main Settings screen.

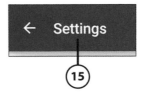

Browser tabs

In this chapter, you discover how to browse the World Wide Web using the browser capabilities of your Android tablet. Topics include the following:

→ Bookmarking websites

→ Sharing websites with your friends

→ Keeping track of sites you have visited

→ Using GPS and browsing together

→ Browsing Incognito

Browsing the Web with Chrome

Your Android tablet has a fully featured web browser called Chrome. In fact, the experience of using the Android tablet's browser is similar to using a desktop browser, just with a smaller screen. You can bookmark sites, hold your Android tablet sideways to fit more onto the screen, and even share your GPS location with websites.

Navigating with Chrome

Let's dive right in and cover how to run the Chrome web browser and use all its features. You can customize the Chrome browser, share your GPS location, bookmark sites, maintain your browsing history, and even access bookmarks stored on your computer.

Get Started with Chrome

1. Tap the Chrome icon.

2. Tap to type a website address or one or more search terms. Some websites move the web page up to hide the address field. When this happens, you can drag the web page down to reveal the address bar again.

3. Tap to open a new browser tab from which you can go to a new website.

4. Tap to bookmark the website that you are currently looking at. If the site is already bookmarked, you can edit the bookmark.

5. Tap to search the Internet by speaking or to say the name of a website you want to go to.

6. Tap to manually refresh the website.

7. Tap the left and right arrows to go to the previous or next page on the current website, or to go to a previous or next website.

8. Tap the Menu icon to see more options, such as finding a word on the web page.

Use Web Page and Chrome Options

While a web page is open, you have a number of options such as finding text on a web page and forcing Chrome to load the desktop version of a website.

1. Tap the Menu icon.

2. Tap to open a new browser tab.

3. Tap to open a new Incognito browser tab.

②

New tab   ⋮ —— **①**

New incognito tab —————— **③**

Bookmarks

Recent tabs

History

Share...

Print...

Find in page

Add to homescreen

Request desktop site   ☐

Settings

Help & feedback

Browse in Secret (Going Incognito)

If you want to visit a website in secret, you can. Visiting a website in secret using an Incognito browser tab means that the site you visit does not appear in your browser history or search history and does not otherwise leave a trace of itself on your Android tablet. To create a new Incognito browser tab, while in the browser tab screen, tap the Menu icon and then tap New Incognito Tab. When you have Incognito tabs open, a new icon appears on the top right that enables you to switch between regular browser tabs and Incognito tabs.

Tap to switch between regular and Incognito tabs

4. Tap to open the Chrome book-marks screen.

5. Tap Recent Tabs to see websites that were recently opened in Chrome browser tabs on your desktop computer and all other devices where you have the Chrome browser installed and running.

6. Tap to see the history of all web-sites you have visited on all devic-es where you run the Chrome web browser.

7. Tap to share the current web page's address using a number of methods, including Facebook, Twitter, Skype, Bluetooth, and Android Beam, or to copy the link to the Clipboard.

8. Tap to print the web page on a printer that is linked to your Google Chrome Cloud Print account, or print the web page to a Portable Document Format (PDF) file.

9. Tap to find a word on the current web page.

10. Tap to add a shortcut for the cur-rent web page on your tablet's Home screen.

11. Tap to request the desktop ver-sion of the current website if you are seeing a mobile version. When you check the box, Chrome refreshes the page with the desk-top version.

12. Tap to change the Chrome web browser settings.

How Can I See My Desktop Computer's Browser Tabs?

To see your desktop computer's Chrome browser tabs, make sure you install Chrome on your desktop computer and use it as your default web browser. When setting up Chrome, use the same Google account as you use on your Android tablet. Then not only are your bookmarks kept in sync between your tablet and desktop (and all other devices where Chrome is installed), but also any browser tabs you have open in Chrome on your desktop computer (called browser windows on the desktop version of Chrome) can be seen as described in Step 5. Even if you close Chrome and shut down your computer, you still see the last tabs that were open.

Master Chrome Browser Tricks

Your Android tablet has some unique tricks to help you browse regular websites on a small screen.

Viewed in portrait

Viewed in landscape

1. Rotate your Android tablet on its side to put the tablet into *landscape orientation*. Your Android tablet automatically switches the screen to landscape mode.

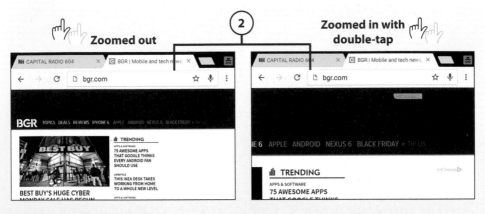

Zoomed out

2

Zoomed in with double-tap

2. Double-tap the screen to zoom in and out.

Zoom with Pinch to Zoom

An alternative way to zoom, which enables you to actually zoom in much further, is to place your thumb and forefinger on the screen and spread them apart to zoom in and then move them back together to zoom out.

Zoomed in with pinch to zoom

3. If menu choices on a web page are too small, when you touch a menu item, the Chrome browser shows you a zoomed in portion of the menu to enable you to more easily touch your menu item.

3

Zoomed in to menu choices

Managing Bookmarks and History

Your Android tablet enables you to bookmark your favorite websites, but it also keeps track of where you have browsed and can show you your browsing history broken up by days, weeks, and months. The history also enables you to read web pages offline.

Open a Bookmark

1. Tap the Menu icon.

2. Tap Bookmarks.

3. Tap to switch between your mobile bookmarks and bookmarks that you have on your desktop computer.

4. Tap a bookmark to open it.

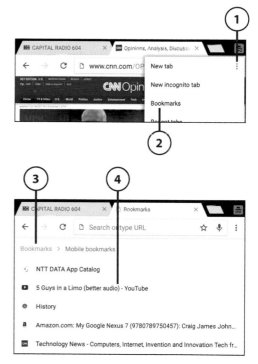

Work with Bookmarks

1. Tap a bookmark to open it in the current tab.

2. Touch and hold a bookmark to see more options.

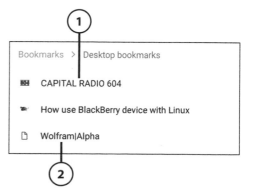

3. Tap to open the bookmark in a new browser tab.

4. Tap to open the bookmark in an Incognito tab (secretive browsing).

5. Tap to edit the bookmark.

6. Tap to delete the bookmark.

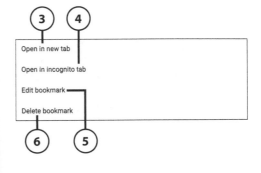

Add a Bookmark

While you are viewing a web page, you can add it to your list of bookmarks.

1. Tap the star icon in the address bar.

2. Change the bookmark name if you want to. It defaults to the web page's title.

3. Edit the web page link if you want to or leave it as is (normally best).

4. Select where to save the bookmark. You can choose to save it in Mobile Bookmarks (only on your tablet) or in one of the bookmark folders that you have synchronized from your desktop computer.

5. Tap to save the bookmark.

Where to Save Bookmarks

When you save bookmarks, you can choose to save them locally or to one of your desktop bookmark folders. If you choose to save a bookmark locally, it is saved only to your Android tablet. The bookmark is not synchronized to the Google Cloud or made available anywhere other than on your tablet. If you choose to save the bookmark to one of your desktop bookmark folders, that bookmark is stored in the Google Cloud and is then available to you on any device where you use that same Google account. This includes when you log in to your Google account on your desktop version of the Chrome browser on your computer and any Android smartphone or tablet that you purchase and use in the future.

Manage Browsing History

Your browsing history is a list of all websites that you have visited. Browsing your history can help find websites you have visited in the past but forgotten about.

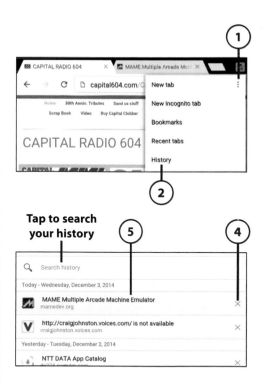

1. Tap the Menu icon.

2. Tap History.

3. Tap Clear Browsing Data at the bottom of the screen to clear all Chrome browser data including browser history, cache, cookies, and saved passwords.

4. Tap the X icon to the right of a browser history item to remove it.

5. Touch and hold an item to see more options for that item.

Tap to search your history

6. Tap to open the website in a new browser tab.

7. Tap to open the website in a new Incognito browser tab.

8. Tap to copy the link for this website to the clipboard.

9. Tap to copy the link's title text to the clipboard.

10. Tap to save the contents of the web page to your tablet. Only the text and layout is saved, not the images. You can find the downloaded web page by opening the Downloads app.

Working with Multiple Open Tabs

As you have seen, you can open multiple browser tabs each with their own websites loaded. As you open more and more tabs, Chrome collapses some of them on the screen to maximize space. To see the collapsed tabs, swipe from left to right or right to left over the tabs and they scroll.

Tabs collapsed to maximize space

Swipe right to reveal collapsed tabs

Customizing Browser Settings

Your Android tablet's Chrome browser is customizable. Here are the different settings you can adjust.

1. Tap the Menu icon.

2. Tap Settings.

3. Tap your Google account.

4. Tap your Google account on the next screen if you have more than one account.

5. Tap to enable or disable synchronization, and choose what to synchronize.

6. Check the box to synchronize everything, or uncheck it to selectively choose what to synchronize.

7. Tap to choose whether you want to encrypt saved passwords using your Google credentials, or encrypt everything using a new pass phrase.

8. Tap to save your changes and return to the account choice screen.

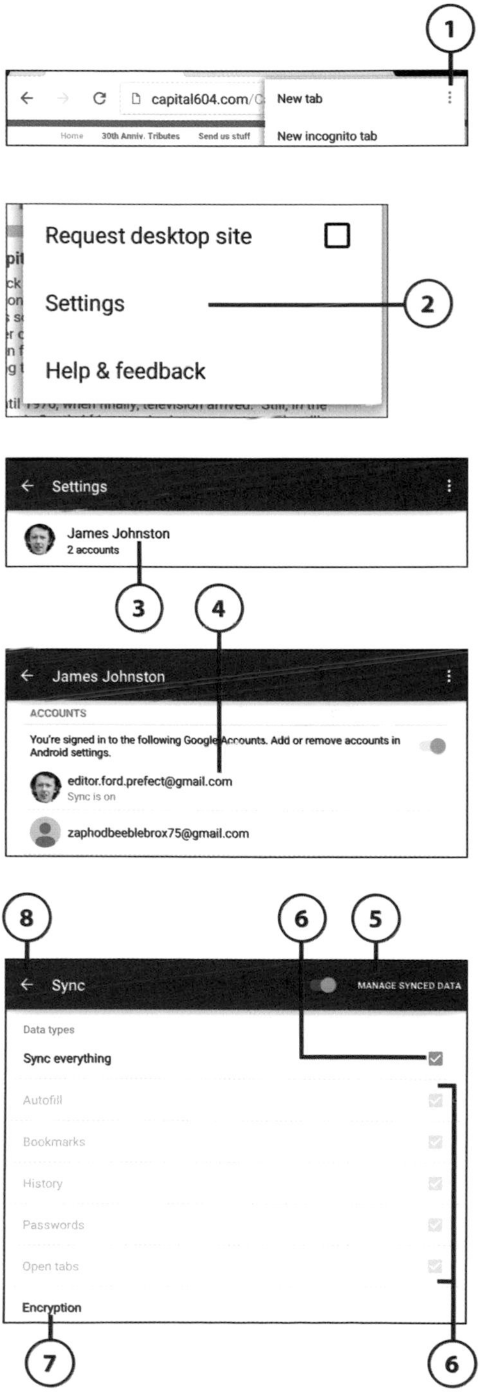

9. Tap to save your changes and return to the main Settings screen.

10. Tap to choose the search engine to use. You can choose Google, Yahoo!, Bing, Ask, or AOL.

11. Tap to enable or disable the Autofill forms feature and create profiles that contain your information and credit card information for Chrome to use in those forms.

12. Tap to enable or disable the capability for Chrome to save your website passwords. This setting also enables you to view and remove any passwords already stored.

13. Tap to see the Privacy settings. Read more about Chrome privacy settings and what information is sent for each setting by going to the website at https://support.google.com/chrome/ and searching for "privacy settings."

14. Tap to clear some or all of your browsing data. This includes your browsing history, browser cache, cookies and other site data, any saved passwords, and any autofill info.

15. Tap to enable or disable Chrome making suggestions of alternatives when you mistype a website address. If enabled, Chrome sends Google what you have typed in the address bar.

16. Tap to enable or disable Chrome making suggestions as you type in the address bar. If enabled, Chrome sends Google what you have typed in the address bar.

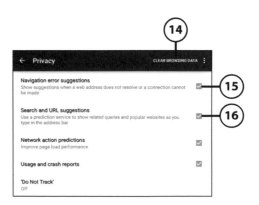

17. Tap to enable or disable the feature where Chrome preloads the IP address of every link on a web page to speed up browsing. If enabled, Chrome sends Google the name of the website you are visiting.

18. Tap to enable or disable sending usage and crash reports. If enabled, Chrome might send personal information to Google.

19. Tap to enable the Do Not Track feature. When enabled, Chrome sends a request that you not be tracked to websites you visit. What the website does with that request is unpredictable, so this feature might not be effective.

20. Tap to save your changes and return to the main Settings screen.

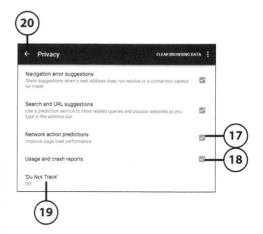

>>>*Go Further*

WHERE DOES MY PERSONAL INFORMATION GO?

In Steps 14–19 of the "Customizing Browser Settings" section, you see options to allow Chrome to send your personal information to Google. In each case the information is either used to make your web browsing experience quicker and easier or to help Google figure out why the Chrome browser is crashing. For example, in Step 18 you can allow Chrome to send information about what you were busy doing when the Chrome web browser crashed (if it crashes in the future). Because debugging software means trying to figure out every possible combination of tasks, it is never possible to come up with every combination unless Google has visibility into how people like you are using the software in the real world. The information that is sent to Google is not shared with anyone and is kept private and confidential, so you will not suddenly start receiving spam emails after Google has received your information.

21. Tap to change the size of text displayed on web pages (text scaling) and to override a website's capability to prevent zooming.

What Is Text Scaling?

When you use text scaling, you instruct your Android tablet to always increase or decrease the font sizes used on a web page by a specific percentage. For example, you can automatically make all text 150% larger than was originally intended.

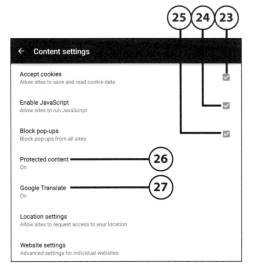

22. Tap to change content settings such as accepting cookies, blocking pop-up ads, and sharing your location.

23. Tap to enable or disable accepting cookies.

24. Tap to enable or disable the capability for Chrome to run JavaScript. This is normally left on because many websites use JavaScript to enhance their site and make it easier to use.

25. Tap to enable or disable blocking web pop-ups.

26. Tap to enable or disable content protection. Having this enabled allows websites to authenticate your tablet so that they can let you watch premium protected videos.

27. Tap to enable or disable Google Translate. When this is enabled, you can translate web pages into other languages.

28. Tap to enable or disable allowing websites to access your location and specify how accurately your location is identified.

29. Tap to browse settings for all websites you have visited so that you can clear any data stored by those individual websites and enable or disable sending your GPS location per website.

30. Tap to save your changes and return to the main Settings screen.

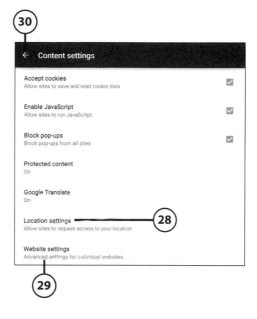

What Are Cookies?

Cookies are small files that are placed on your tablet by websites. They contain information that might enhance your browsing experience if you return to the website from which they came. For example, they could contain information about what pages you visited before and your browsing history on the website. When you return to the website that placed the cookie, it can read the information in the cookie. Cookies can contain any kind of information, so it is possible for them to be used maliciously, although it's not likely.

How Does Pop-Up Blocking Work?

When you enable pop-up blocking, your Android tablet automatically blocks any website request to pop up a window. This is good because almost every pop-up on a website is some kind of scam to get you to tap a link so that you go to a new site. Sometimes, though, pop-ups are legitimate, and a website that needs you to allow pop-ups will ask you to allow them. You can disable the pop-up blocker anytime and then re-enable it when you stop using that website. Unlike desktop computers, you cannot temporarily stop blocking pop-ups, so you need to remember to manually disable and enable the pop-up blocker.

31. Tap Reduce Data Usage to allow Google servers to compress the data coming from websites so that it reduces how much data it takes to load each web page.

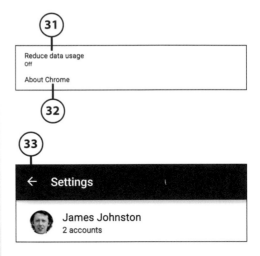

How Does Reduce Data Usage Work?

When you enable Reduce Data Usage, behind the scenes a setting is changed so that every web page you visit (with the exception of secure web pages and web pages opened in an Incognito tab) are re-routed via the Google servers before proceeding to your tablet. This is called a Proxy, and it means that the Google servers act like a proxy for your web data. Although this feature does reduce the size of web pages being downloaded, the way it does it is by compressing images so that they look washed out and end up at a lower resolution.

32. Tap to see technical information about the Chrome browser.

33. Tap to save your changes and return to the Chrome main screen.

Click an Email Address to Send an Email

If you see an email address on a web page, tap it to compose a new email to that email address. The first time you do this you may be prompted to choose which email app you want to use. After you have selected the app, you can touch Always to let Chrome remember your selection.

Choose which email app to use

Take Actions on a Link

If you touch and hold a link on a website, you can choose to open it in a new tab, open it in an Incognito tab (secretive browsing), copy the link's address (to paste into another app, such as an email you are composing), and save the link (and its associated web page) as a file on your tablet.

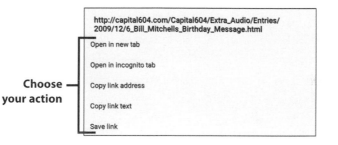

Choose your action —

> http://capital604.com/Capital604/Extra_Audio/Entries/
> 2009/12/6_Bill_Mitchells_Birthday_Message.html
>
> Open in new tab
>
> Open in incognito tab
>
> Copy link address
>
> Copy link text
>
> Save link

>>>Go Further

MY TABLET DOESN'T HAVE CHROME

Some Android tablets do not come pre-loaded with the Chrome web browser, but they do have a built-in web browser simply called Internet. Most of the steps in this chapter will apply to the Internet web browser, with a few variations. For example, the way that browser tabs are handled is a bit different. Instead of tabs appearing across the top of the web browser, there is an icon that indicates the number of tabs you have open; when you tap it, you can switch between tabs and create new tabs or new Incognito tabs. Some versions of the Internet web browser don't have the star icon that allows you to bookmark a page. To book-mark a page in these instances, tap the Menu icon and tap the plus icon.

Internet browser

Incognito tab

Manage tabs

Add Bookmark

Search Google

See your
teams

In this chapter, you find out how to use Google Maps, Navigation, and Google Now. Topics include:

→ Google Maps
→ Navigation
→ Google Now
→ Taking map data offline

Google Now and Navigation

You can use your Android tablet as a GPS navigation device while you walk or drive around. Your tablet also includes an app called Google Now that provides all the information you need when you need it.

Google Now

You can access Google Now from the lock screen or from any screen, which enables you to search the Internet. Google Now provides you with information such as how long it takes to drive to work and the scores from your favorite teams.

Access Google Now

You can access Google Now from any app or the Home screen by swiping from the bottom bezel up onto the screen and toward the word Google.

**Swipe up from
the bottom bezel**

1. Cards automatically appear based on your settings. Examples of these cards are scores for the sports teams you follow, upcoming meetings, weather in the location where you work, and traffic on the way to work.

2. Tap the microphone icon to speak a search or to command Google Now to do something. You can also type your search terms.

3. Information relevant to your search appears.

Commanding Google Now

In addition to searching the Internet using Google Now, you can command Google Now to do things for you. For example, you can tell Google Now to set an alarm for you, compose a text message, or even send an email. This is just a small list of the types of things you can have Google Now do for you. To see a comprehensive list of commands, visit http://trendblog.net/list-of-google-now-voice-commands-infographic/.

Setting an alarm

Set Up Google Now

For Google Now to work for you, you need to set it up correctly. This also means sharing your location information with Google.

1. Swipe in from the left bezel to reveal the menu.

2. Tap Settings.

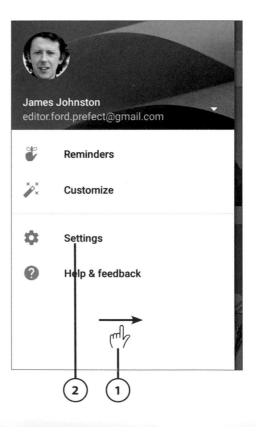

3. Tap to turn Google Now on or off.

4. Tap to manage what Google Now can search for. This can include apps you have installed, bookmarks and web history in the Chrome web browser, your contacts, Google Play Books, Movies & TV, and Music.

5. Tap Voice to manage how and when Google Now responds to your voice.

6. Tap to choose the languages that Google Now responds to.

7. Tap to choose when Google Now speaks back to you. Your choices are On (which means always), Off (which means never), or only when you are using a hands-free device (such as a Bluetooth headset or your car's built-in Bluetooth connection).

8. Tap to choose when your Google Now should be listening for you to say "OK Google," which is the key phrase that launches Google Now. You can choose to have Google Now listening only from the Google Now app, from any screen, or from the lock screen.

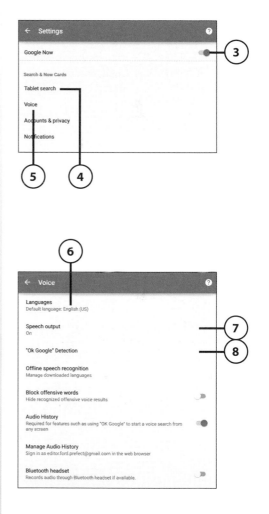

Commanding Google Now

Be careful about deciding when Google Now can listen for commands. If you allow Google Now to listen for "OK Google" on any screen (which means on any screen plus while running any app), the only drawback could be battery life suffering, but if you let Google Now listen for "OK Google" from the lock screen, there is the potential for someone else to instruct your tablet to do things. Even though when you enable this feature, you are asked to say "OK Google" three times so that Google Now can become familiar with your voice, it is possible for others to command your tablet to send emails, read emails back to them, and so on.

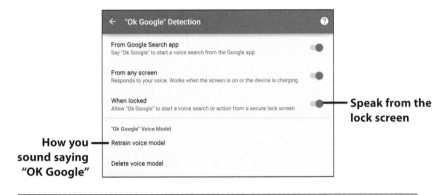

Speak from the lock screen

How you sound saying "OK Google"

9. Tap to manage whether Google Now can work even when there is no Internet connection. This is achieved by downloading one or more languages to your tablet.

10. Tap to block offensive words being spoken when search results are returned by voice.

11. Tap to allow Google Now to keep a running history of what you say. If you disable this, Google Now cannot listen for you to say "OK Google."

12. Tap to manage your audio history. This includes the capability to play back what Google Now heard you say, and delete individual things you have previously said.

13. Tap to allow Google Now to record your voice using your Bluetooth headset or built-in car Bluetooth.

14. Tap to save your changes and return to the main Google Now settings screen.

15. Tap Accounts & Privacy.

(14)

← Voice   ?

Languages
Default language: English (US)

Speech output
On

"Ok Google" Detection

Offline speech recognition
Manage downloaded languages

Block offensive words
Hide recognized offensive voice results

Audio History
Required for features such as using "OK Google" to start a voice search from any screen

Manage Audio History
Sign in as editor.ford.prefect@gmail.com in the web browser

Bluetooth headset
Records audio through Bluetooth headset if available.   (13)

← Settings   ?

Google Now

Search & Now Cards

Tablet search

Voice

Accounts & privacy

Notifications

(15)

16. Tap to choose which of your Google accounts (if you have more than one) you want to use for Google Now.

17. Tap to choose whether you want to share your Commute status, such as when you leave for home or leave for work. People need to be in your Google+ Circles to receive your Commute updates.

18. Tap to enable or disable the capability for Google to track your location. After this option is enabled, you can set how accurately your location is reported.

19. Tap to enable or disable Web History. Web History shows everything you have done on the Internet using this tablet. Turning Web History off may disable Google Now.

20. Tap to see your Web History. This enables you to see everything you have searched for, pictures and videos you have looked at, and even the ads that have displayed on the screen.

21. Tap enable or disable Personal Results, which are bits of information personal to you that can be found in your Google account, such as Google Calendar, Gmail account, and Google+. Keeping this enabled allows Google Now to search your personal information.

22. Tap to manage whether apps can share your data with Google and clear any data that apps on your tablet have shared with Google.

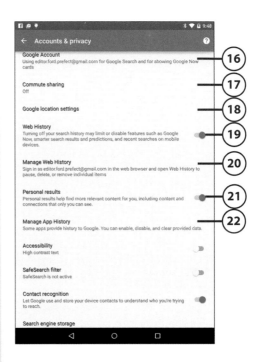

23. Tap to enable or disable high contrast text if you have a vision disability.

24. Tap to enable or disable the SafeSearch Filter that blocks offensive content.

25. Tap to enable or disable Google Now having access to your contacts. When this is enabled, you can do extra tasks, such as send text messages and emails to people.

26. Tap to manage your search engine storage. Google provides a local search engine that apps can use to provide better searching. This screen enables you to see which apps are using it, and you can also clear the data from it.

27. Tap to save your changes and return to the main Google Now settings screen.

28. Tap to manage if Google Now alerts you—and in the case of urgent alerts like public alerts, reminders, unusual traffic, and time to leave for appointments— what ring tone is played and whether your tablet also vibrates when the alert sounds.

29. Tap to save your changes and return to Google Now.

Tell Google Maps Where You Live and Work

Google Now can be even more effective if you configure your work and home addresses in Google Maps. Google Now then uses that information to tell you things like how long your commute to work will be, whether there is heavy traffic on the route, and so on. See Step 3 in the "Configure Google Maps Settings" task later in this chapter on how to do that.

Google Maps

Google Maps enables you to see where you are on a map, find points of interest close to you, get driving or walking directions, and review extra layers of information, such as a satellite view.

1. Tap to launch Google Maps.

2. Tap to type a search term, the name of a business, or an address.

3. Tap to speak a search term, the name of a business, or an address.

4. Tap to get walking or driving directions from one location to another. You can also choose to use public transit or biking paths to get to your destination.

5. Tap to switch between the top-down view that always points North, and the 3D view that follows the direction your tablet is pointing.

6. Tap to switch between the map view and satellite view.

7. Tap to explore what's around your current location.

8. Swipe in from the left of the screen to reveal the menu.

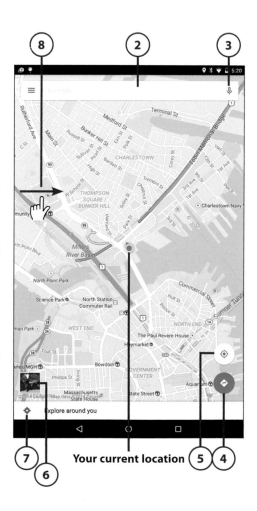

Your current location

9. Tap to switch to a different Google account for use with Google Maps.

10. Tap to see your work and home address, plus addresses you have recently searched for.

11. Tap to toggle between the map view and the satellite view.

12. Tap to show the current traffic conditions on the map or satellite view.

13. Tap to show all public transport locations on the map view or satellite view.

14. Tap to show all bicycling routes on the map view or satellite view.

15. Tap to see the terrain view.

16. Tap to launch the Google Earth app.

17. Touch to change the settings for Google Maps.

18. Touch to explore what's nearby.

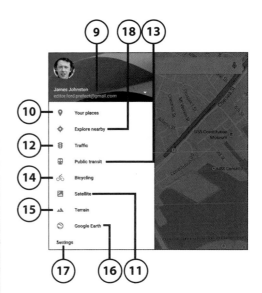

Changing Google Maps Settings

See the "Configure Google Maps Settings" task later in this chapter for more information about customizing Google Maps.

Get Directions

You can use Google Maps to get directions to where you want to go.

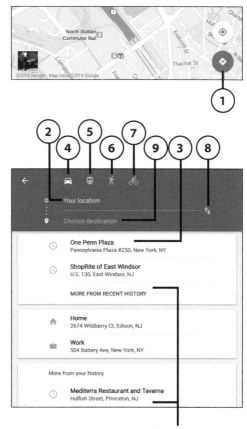

1. Tap the Directions icon.

2. Tap to set the starting point or leave it as Your Location (which is where you are now).

3. Tap to flip the start and end points.

4. Tap to use driving directions.

5. Tap to use public transportation.

Public Transportation

If you choose to use public transportation to get to your destination, you have two extra options to use. You can choose the type of public transportation to use, including bus, subway, train, or tram/light rail. You can also choose the best route (fewer transfers and less walking).

Scroll to see more previous destinations

6. Tap to walk to your destination.

7. Tap to use bike paths (if available).

8. Tap to choose a previous destination. If you need to type the address of your destination, skip to Step 9; if not, skip to Step 10.

9. Type or speak the destination address.

10. Tap to make changes to your route, including choosing alternative routes to travel, and modify options like avoiding toll roads. If you are happy with the route as-is, skip to Step 14.

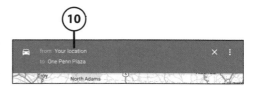

11. Tap to decide whether you want to avoid highways, tolls, or ferries.

12. Tap to choose an alternative route. If you choose an alternative route, the screen will automatically return to the map view.

13. Tap to return to the map view.

14. Tap to start the navigation.

15. Tap to see and select alternative routes as they appear on the map.

16. Tap the Menu icon to mute the voice guidance, show traffic conditions, choose the satellite view, and show the entire route alternatives.

17. Tap to speak commands like "Show alternative route," "How's traffic ahead," or "What time will I get there."

18. Tap to cancel the route.

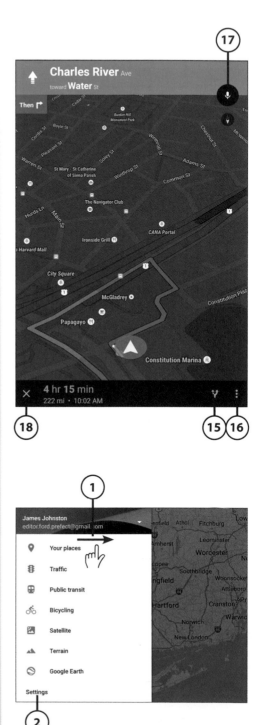

Configure Google Maps Settings

1. Swipe in from the left side of the screen.

2. Tap Settings.

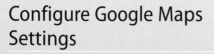

3. Tap to edit your work and home addresses. Telling Maps your home and work addresses is important for Google Now to work more efficiently, but it also helps you quickly plan new routes to work and home.

4. Tap to enable or disable the capability for your tablet to report its location. You can also choose the accuracy of your location by changing the mode.

5. Tap to improve your location accuracy if you think that your tablet is not reporting it correctly.

6. Tap to see addresses you have looked up and received directions to. You can also delete items in this list.

7. Tap to set the distance unit of measure. You can either set it to automatic so that Google Maps adjusts it based on where you are on the planet, or you can manually set it.

8. Tap to save your changes and return to the main Google Maps screen.

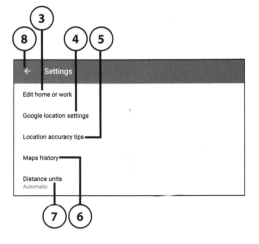

Use Offline Google Maps

Google Maps enables you to download small parts of the global map to your tablet. This is useful if you are traveling and need an electronic map but cannot connect to a network to download it in real time.

1. Swipe in from the left of the screen.

2. Tap Your Places.

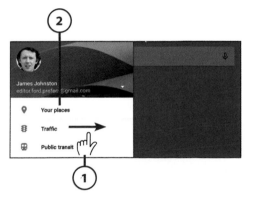

3. Scroll down to the bottom of the Your Places screen, and tap View All and Manage.

4. Tap Save a New Offline Map.

5. Pan around to find the area of the map you want to save offline.

6. Pinch to zoom out or unpinch to zoom in to the area of the map you want to save offline.

7. Tap Save This Map when the area of the map fills the screen.

8. Type a name for the offline map and tap Save.

How Much Map Can I Take Offline?

When selecting the area of the map to take offline, you are limited to approximately 100 Mb of map data. You don't need to worry about the size of the data because if you have selected an area that is too large, Google Maps gives you a warning.

Your selection area is too large warning

It's Not All Good

Offline Maps Have Limited Use

If you download some map data to your tablet, you can use it to zoom in and out of the area you downloaded and also see where you are on the map in real time even though you have no network coverage. You cannot, however, get directions within the downloaded map area or use the Navigation app to get turn-by-turn directions. You also cannot search for things in the down-loaded map area or see points of interest.

So how useful is having map data already downloaded to your tablet? Because offline maps are already downloaded, they help when you have a network connection and are getting driving directions because Google Maps does not need to download the map data in real time, which could save you a lot of money in data roaming charges.

Tap to see Day, Week,
or Month views

Tap to add a new
appointment

In this chapter, you find out how to set the time, use the Clock application, and use the Calendar application. Topics include the following:

→ Synchronizing to the correct time
→ Working with the Clock application
→ Setting alarms
→ Working with the Calendar

Working with Date, Time, and Calendar

Your Android tablet has a Clock application that you can use as a bedside alarm. The Calendar application synchronizes to your Google or corporate calendars and enables you to create meetings while on the road and to always know where your next meeting is.

Setting the Date and Time

Before you start working with the Clock and Calendar applications, you need to make sure that your Android tablet has the correct date and time.

1. Pull down the Quick Settings Bar and tap Settings.

2. Tap Date & Time under System.

3. Tap to enable or disable synchronizing time and date with the Internet. It is best to leave this enabled.

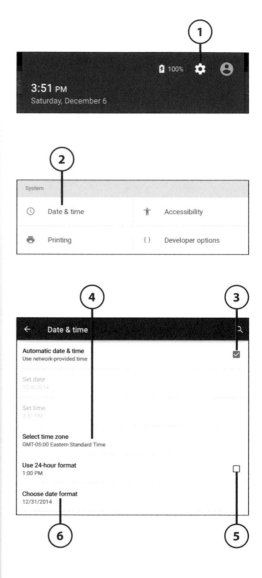

Does Network Time Sync Always Work?

Your tablet updates its clock from the Internet. As long as you have a Wi-Fi or cellular data connection and your time zone is correctly selected, your clock should stay up to date. If you don't connect to the Internet for a long time, don't worry; your clock remains accurate within one second or two.

4. Tap to choose your time zone. This should already be set correctly, but check it anyway.

5. Tap to enable or disable the use of 24-hour time format. This makes your Android tablet represent time without a.m. or p.m. For example 1:00 p.m. becomes 13:00.

6. Tap to change the way in which the date is represented. Leaving it set to Regional allows your tablet to modify how the date is displayed based on the region you are in (using your GPS location), or you can manually set it.

Clock Application

The Clock application is preinstalled on your Android tablet and provides the functionality of a bedside clock and alarm clock.

Navigate the Clock Application

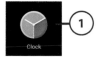

1. Tap the Clock icon.

2. Tap to manage alarms.

3. Rotate your Android tablet onto its side to increase the size of the digits.

4. Tap the Menu icon to change the Clock app's settings and activate Night mode. When Night mode is active, the screen becomes dim until you touch it.

5. Tap to manage which extra cities you want to see time for.

6. Tap to use the stop watch function.

7. Tap to use the timer function.

8. Tap to see the main clock screen (the clock shown in the figure).

Manage Alarms

The Clock app enables you to set multiple alarms. These can be one-time alarms or recurring alarms. Even if you exit the Clock app, the alarms you set still trigger.

1. Tap to manage your alarms.

2. Tap an existing alarm to edit it. Skip to Step 5 for instructions on editing the alarm details.

3. Tap the on/off switch to enable or disable an existing alarm.

4. Tap to add a new alarm.

5. Tap the hour you want your alarm to trigger. After you tap an hour, the screen automatically changes.

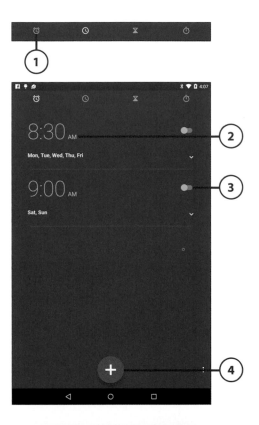

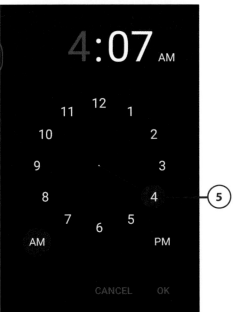

6. Tap the minutes past the hour you want your alarm to trigger. You can also drag the purple minute selector to choose a more precise time.

7. Tap AM or PM.

8. Tap OK to continue setting the alarm's extra settings.

9. Tap to set a name for your alarm.

10. Tap to choose a ringtone to play when the alarm triggers.

11. Tap to choose whether you want your new alarm to be repeated. If the Repeat check box is selected, the days of the week appear below it. Select the days of the week you want your alarm to repeat.

12. Tap the up arrow to save the alarm.

Drag to be more precise

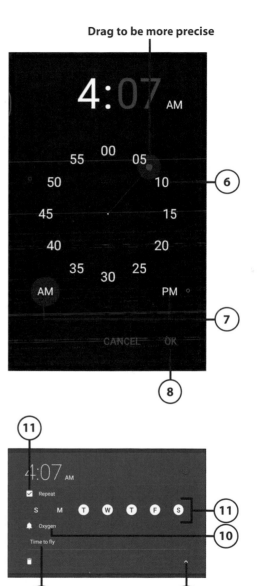

Adjust Clock Settings

Use the Settings to adjust the settings for the Clock app and control how all alarms function.

1. Tap the Menu icon.

2. Tap Settings.

3. Tap to choose whether you want the clock style to be digital or analog.

4. Check the box if you want a new clock to be automatically added for your home town when you travel.

5. Tap to change your home city's time zone.

6. Tap to set how long the alarm plays before it automatically silences itself. Your choices range from 5 minutes to 30 minutes; alternatively, you can set it to Never so that the alarm plays until you wake up and dismiss it.

7. Tap to set the duration of the snooze period. Your choices range between 5 and 30 minutes.

8. Tap to set the volume for all alarms.

9. Tap to set how the volume buttons behave if you press either of them when the alarm sounds. Your choices are Do Nothing, Snooze, and Dismiss.

10. Tap to save the settings and return to the Clock main screen.

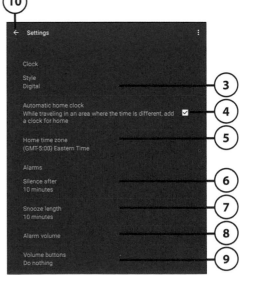

Using the Calendar Application

The Calendar application enables you to synchronize all of your Google Calendars and calendars from other accounts like your work calendar and any personal calendars to your Android tablet. You can accept appointments and create and modify appointments right on your tablet. Any changes are automatically synchronized wirelessly back to each calendar service.

Get to Know the Calendar Main Screen

The main screen of the Calendar app shows a 1-day, 1-week, or 1-month view of your appointments. The Calendar app also shows events from multiple calendars at the same time.

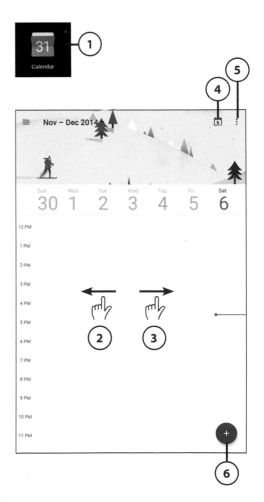

1. Tap the Calendar icon.

2. Swipe left to go backward in time.

3. Swipe right to go forward in time.

4. Tap to jump to today's date.

5. Tap to search the calendar for an event and choose the calendar view. You can choose from the month, week, day, and agenda views.

6. Tap to create a new calendar event.

Event Colors

The Calendar app can display one calendar or many calendars at the same time. If you choose to display multiple calendars, events from each calendar are color coded so that you can tell which events are from which calendar.

Chapter 7

Adjust Calendar Settings

In this section you find out how to tweak the Calendar app and how to choose which calendars are synchronized to your tablet.

1. Swipe in from the left bezel to reveal the menu.

2. Tap a calendar to show or hide it. When it is hidden, all events from that calendar are not visible. Some account types can only have one calendar while others can have many.

3. Tap Settings.

4. Tap General.

editor.ford.prefect@gmail.com

Events

Consulting

zaphodbeeblebrox75@gmail.c..

Events

Author Schedule

fprefect@humanoidsoftware.on..

fprefect@humanoidsoftware.o..

More

Birthdays

Holidays

Settings

Help & feedback

← Settings

General

Events from Gmail

5. Tap to set the first day of your week. You can choose Saturday, Sunday, or Monday. You can also choose Locale Default so that the locale you have set in the device settings determines what the first day of the week is. See Chapter 9, "Customizing Your Android Tablet," for more information on setting the device locale.

6. Tap to enable or disable using the current time zone that you and your tablet are in when displaying the calendar and event times. When this is disabled, the time zone you choose in Step 7 is always used instead of using the local time zone you are traveling in.

7. Tap to set the time zone you want your tablet to use when you have disabled "Use Device Time Zone" in Step 6.

8. Tap to enable or disable showing events that you have already declined in your calendar.

9. Tap to enable or disable showing the seasonal illustration on the main calendar screen.

10. Tap to set the default event length time when you create a new event in your Google calendar. This setting does not affect non-Google calendars.

11. Tap to enable or disable receiving notifications for calendar events.

12. Tap to choose the ringtone to play when you are being alerted for calendar events.

13. Tap to edit your Quick Responses.

14. Tap to save your changes and return to the main Settings screen.

What Are Quick Responses?

Let's say that you are running late for a meeting. When the meeting reminder appears on your tablet and you know that you are running late, you can choose to use a predefined Quick Response, such as "Be there in 10 minutes" or "Go ahead and start without me." When you choose a Quick Response, your tablet emails that response to all meeting participants. See how to use Quick Responses in the next section.

15. Tap to choose to whether you want events you receive in your Gmail account like flight details, concert details, or a restaurant reservation to be automatically added to your calendar.

16. Tap to choose whether to include birthdays from your Google account on your calendar.

17. Tap to choose whether you want to include national holidays on your calendar, and the country those holidays are in.

18. Tap a calendar to choose the color that it uses, and change the default notifications you want to receive when an event is coming up.

19. Tap to return to the Calendar app.

(19) (15) (18)

← Settings

General

Events from Gmail

editor.ford.prefect@gmail.com

● Events

● Consulting

zaphodbeeblebrox75@gmail.com

● Events

● Author Schedule

fprefect@humanoidsoftware.onmicrosoft.com

● fprefect@humanoidsoftware.onmicrosoft.com

More

● Birthdays

● Holidays

(17) (16)

Use Quick Responses

If you are running late to a meeting, you can send a Quick Response to all meeting participants directly from the meeting reminder.

1. Pull down the Notification Bar.

2. Tap Email Guests.

How to Expand an Alert

If you do not see Snooze and Email Guests you can expand the alert by placing your two fingers on the alert and pulling down. Expanding alerts work on all kinds of alerts, including email alerts. If you see the alert on your lock screen, before unlocking your tablet you can use two fingers to swipe down the alert to use Quick Responses.

---

3. Tap one of the predefined Quick Responses.

4. Tap Send.

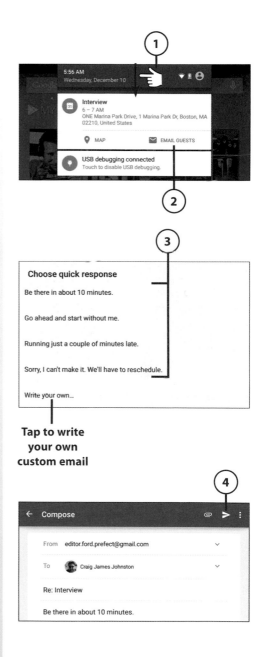

Tap to write your own custom email

Add a New Event

While you're on the road you can add a new appointment or an event, and you can even invite people to it. Events you add synchronize to your Google and corporate calendars in real time (or when you next connect to a network).

1. Tap to add a new event.

2. Tap to change the calendar to create the event in (if you use multiple calendars).

3. Tap to enter a title, place, and people for your event.

4. Type the title of your new event.

5. Tap to enter where the event will take place. This can be a full physical address, which is useful because most smartphones and tablets can map the address. As you type the Calendar app will make suggestions. If you see a suggestion, tap it.

6. Tap to choose who the event will be with. As you type names, the Calendar app will make suggestions from your Contacts. If you see a suggested person, tap them to add them to the event.

Adding People to the Event Does Not Invite Them

Strangely, even if you choose people in Step 6, while their names are shown in the event title, they are not automatically added to the invite list. You will need to manually add them to the event in Step 11 otherwise they will not receive invitations to your event.

Alternatively, you can tap a day or time; then tap it again after it highlights

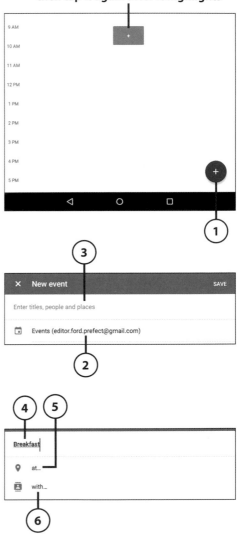

7. Set the start date and time of the event.

8. Set the end date and time of the event.

9. Tap to mark the event as an all-day event.

10. Tap to select whether the meeting repeats. You can make it repeat daily, weekly, or monthly, but you can also set a meeting to repeat—for example, monthly but only every last Thursday. Tapping here also allows you to choose the time zone the meeting will be held in. This is useful if you will be traveling to the meeting in a different time zone.

11. Enter the event guests or event invitees. As you type names, your Android tablet retrieves matching names from your Contacts and your corporate directory.

12. Choose how you want to be reminded. You can choose to be notified on the device as you are for all other notifications or via email. You can choose to be notified multiple times before the event starts.

13. Tap to save the event. Any attendees that you have added are automatically sent an event invitation.

Change event color

Privacy and Availability for Corporate Calendars

If you are creating a new event using your corporate calendar you can tap Calendar default to choose if the event you are creating is public (anyone in your company can see it) or private (only you and the invitees can see it). You can also choose how you appear during the event by tapping Busy. You can choose to appear as busy or available.

Editing and Deleting Events

To edit or delete a calendar event, tap the event, and tap the pencil icon to edit the event. While editing tap Delete at the bottom of the screen to delete the event. When you successfully delete an event that you previously accepted, the Calendar application sends an event decline notice to the event organizer. If you originally created the meeting and it has guests, a meeting cancelation notice is sent to them automatically when you delete it.

Tap to edit ⟶

Respond to an Event Invitation

When you are invited to an event, you can choose your response right on your Android tablet.

1. Tap the new event. It will appear with an outline as opposed to a solid box.

2. Tap Yes, Maybe, or No to indicate whether you will be attending.

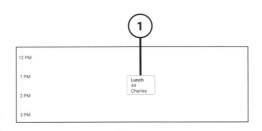

See the top
free apps

Search
for apps

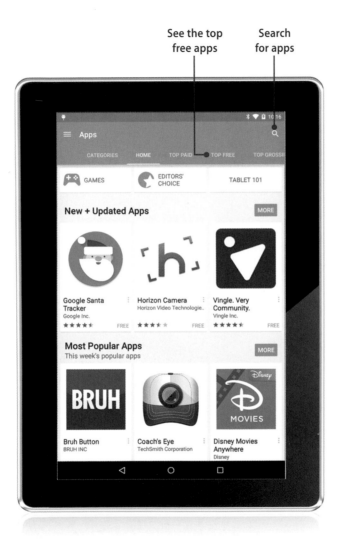

In this chapter, you find out how to purchase and use Android applications on your Android tablet. Topics include the following:

→ Finding applications with Google Play
→ Purchasing applications
→ Keeping applications up to date

Working with Android Applications

Your Android tablet comes with enough applications to make it a worthy tablet. However, wouldn't it be great to play games, update your Facebook and Twitter statuses, or even keep a grocery list? Well, you can use the Google Play store to find these types of applications. Read on to discover how to find, purchase, and maintain applications.

Configuring Google Wallet

Before you start buying applications in the Google Play app, you must first set up your Google Wallet account. If you plan to download only free applications, you do not need a Google Wallet account.

1. From a desktop computer or your Android tablet, open the web browser and go to http://wallet.google.com. Sign in using the same Google account you used to set up your tablet.

2. Click or tap Payment Methods.

3. Click or tap Add a Payment Method, and select either Add a Credit or Debit Card, or Link a Bank Account.

4. Enter the required information to add your payment method.

Navigating Google Play

The Google Play store is the place where you can search for and buy Android applications for your tablet.

1. Tap the Play Store icon.

2. Swipe in from the left of the screen to see Google Play store actions.

3. Tap to see any apps you have already purchased or downloaded.

4. Tap to select which Google account you want to use when you use the Google Play store (if you have multiple Google accounts).

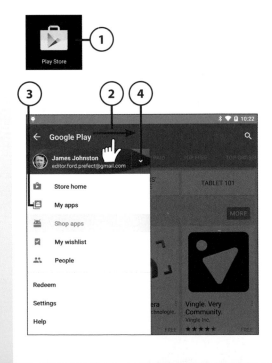

5. Tap to see your Wishlist. This list shows all apps, music, books, and movies that you have placed on your Wishlist.

6. Tap to see people you know on Google+ and see the apps they like.

7. Tap to redeem a Google Play gift card.

8. Tap to change the settings for Google Play. See the "Adjust Google Play Settings" section later in this chapter for more information.

9. Tap anywhere outside the menu to return to the Play store main screen.

10. Tap Apps to see only Android apps.

11. Swipe left and right to move between different top app lists including Top Paid apps, Top Free apps, and Top New apps.

12. Tap to search the Google Play store. This searches everything available in the store, including apps, music, movies, and books.

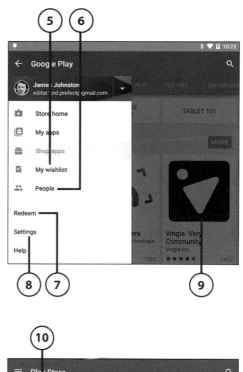

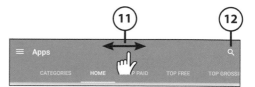

13. Tap Categories to see apps organized by Category.

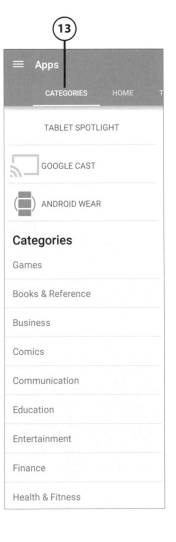

Install Free Applications

You don't have to spend money to get quality applications. Some of the best applications are free.

1. Tap the free application you want to install.

2. Scroll down to read about the app's features, reviews by other people who installed it, and information on the person or company who wrote it. Scrolling down also enables you to share a link to the app with friends.

3. Swipe left and right on the app screen shots to see all of them.

4. Tap Install to download and install the app.

5. Tap to accept the app permissions, and proceed with the installation.

Beware of Permissions

Each time you download a free app or purchase an app from Google Play, you are prompted to accept the app permissions. App permissions are permissions the app wants to have to use features and functions on your Android tablet, such as access to the wireless network or access to your phone log. Pay close attention to the kinds of permissions each app is requesting, and make sure they are appropriate for the type of functionality that the app provides. For example, an app that tests network speed will likely ask for permission to access your wireless network, but if it also asks to access your list of contacts, it might mean that the app is malware and just wants to steal your contacts.

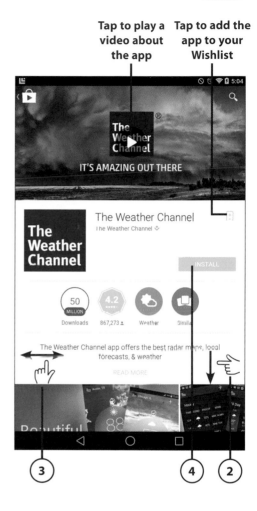

Tap to play a video about the app

Tap to add the app to your Wishlist

Permissions the app is requesting to your tablet

Buy Applications

If an application is not free, the price displays next to the application icon. If you want to buy the application, remember that you need to have a Google Wallet account. See the "Configuring Google Wallet" section earlier in the chapter for more information.

1. Tap the application you want to buy.

What if the Currency Is Different?

When you browse applications in the Google Play store, you might see applications that have prices in foreign currencies, such as in Euros. When you purchase an application, the currency is simply converted into your local currency using the exchange rate at the time of purchase.

2. Scroll down to read the application features, reviews by other people who installed it, and information on the person or company who wrote the application. Scrolling down also enables you to share a link to the app with friends.

3. Swipe left and right on the app screen shots to see all of them.

4. Tap the price to purchase the app.

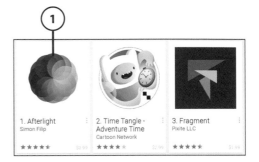

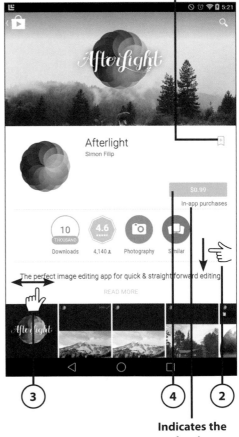

Tap to add the app to your Wishlist

Indicates the app has in-app purchases

What Are In-App Purchases?

An app you install that is either free or costs little may offer extra features that you need to pay for later if you want to take advantage of them. For example, an app might provide ways to edit photos and add effects to them, but some effects are not available until you pay extra for them. This is considered an in-app purchase.

5. Tap to accept the app's requested permissions and proceed to the payment screen.

6. Tap Buy to accept the terms and conditions of purchase.

7. Enter your Google password to validate that it is you who wants to purchase the app.

8. Tap the check box if you don't want to be asked to type your password for every app purchase.

9. Tap to purchase the app. You receive an email from the Google Play store after you purchase an app. The email serves as your invoice.

Permissions the app is requesting to your tablet

Afterlight
needs access to

In-app purchases

Location

Photos/Media/Files

Camera/Microphone

Google play   ACCEPT

(5)

Tap to change the payment method

Afterlight $0.99
Visa-

By tapping "Buy", you agree to the Google Wallet Terms of Service.

Google play   BUY

(7)   (6)

Confirm password
editor.ford.prefect@gmail.com

Google password   (?)

NEVER ASK ME AGAIN

Google play   CONFIRM

(8)   (9)

Manage Apps

Use the My Apps section of Google Play to update apps, delete them, or install apps that you have previously purchased.

1. Swipe in from the left of the screen.

2. Tap My Apps.

3. Tap All to see all apps that are currently installed or previously were installed on all your Android devices.

4. FREE indicates a free app that you previously installed, but that is not installed on this tablet. Tapping the app enables you to install it again for free.

5. PURCHASED indicates an app you previously purchased and installed, but that is no longer installed on this tablet. Tapping the app enables you to install it again for free.

Tap to see only apps you have installed on this device

Tap to update all apps

Tap each app to update it

Allow an App to Be Automatically Updated

When the developer of an app you have installed updates it to fix bugs or add new functionality, you are normally notified of this in the System Tray so that you can manually update the app. Google Play enables you to choose to have the app automatically updated without your intervention. To do this, open the My Apps screen, and touch the app you want to update automatically. Tap the Menu icon and make sure that Auto-Update is checked. Automatic Updating is suspended if the developer of the app changes the permissions that the app requires to function. This enables you to review them and manually update the app.

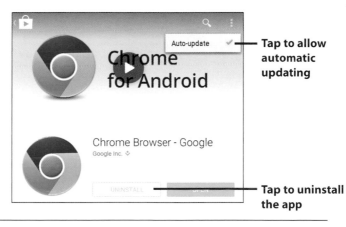

Tap to allow automatic updating

Tap to uninstall the app

Uninstalling an App

When you uninstall an app, you remove the app and its data from your Android tablet. Although the app no longer resides on your Android tablet, you can reinstall it as described in Steps 4 and 5 because the app remains tied to your Google account.

Adjust Google Play Settings

1. Swipe in from the left of the screen.

2. Tap Settings.

3. Check the box to enable notifications of app or game updates.

4. Tap to enable or disable setting all apps you install to automatically update themselves.

5. Check the box to create an app shortcut icon to appear on your Home screen for each app that you install.

6. Tap to clear the Google Play Search History.

7. Tap to adjust or set your content filtering level (for example, apps for everyone, or apps with medium maturity content, and so on). Use this to filter out apps, movies, music, or books that you deem to be inappropriate.

8. Tap to choose whether you want to enter your Google password for every Google Play store purchase, or only every 30 minutes. If you choose 30 minutes, you can purchase content in the store for 30 minutes without typing your password. After 30 minutes have elapsed, you are prompted to enter your password for your next purchase.

9. Tap to return to the main Google Play screen.

Accidentally Uninstall an Application?

What if you accidentally uninstall an application or you uninstalled an application in the past but now decide you'd like to use it again? To get the application back, go to the My Apps view in Google Play. Scroll to that application and tap it. Tap Install to reinstall it.

Install Apps Not from the Google Play Store

Although it is not recommended that you install Android apps not found in the Google Play store, there is a way to do it. Open Settings, tap Security, and tap the switch next to Unknown Sources. If you use your tablet for work, your company's Mobile Device Management (MDM) system will likely require this setting to be enabled so that it can push down the MDM Agent app and enable you to install your company's internal apps.

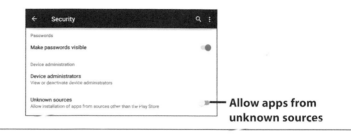

Allow apps from unknown sources

Other App Stores

If you have a Samsung Galaxy tablet, you will find an additional app store icon called Galaxy Apps. This is an app store run by Samsung. It uses its own, separate method of billing, so you will not be able to use your existing Google Wallet account. Although the Galaxy App store is separate, it doesn't have anything that isn't already in the Google Play Store. The only difference is that apps made by Samsung might be updated more quickly in the Galaxy App store than the Google Play Store.

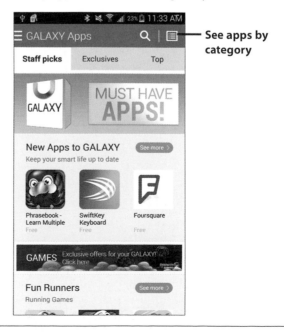

See apps by category

Choose a new wallpaper

Set wallpaper

In this chapter, you discover how to customize your Android tablet to suit your needs and lifestyle. Topics include the following:

→ Using wallpapers and live wallpapers
→ Replacing the keyboard
→ Adding widgets
→ Changing sound and display settings
→ Setting region and language

9

Customizing Your Android Tablet

Your Android tablet arrives preconfigured to appeal to most buyers; however, you might want to change the way some of the features work or personalize it to fit your mood or lifestyle. Luckily your Android tablet is customizable.

You can add useful widgets to your Home screen that provide real-time information, change your wallpaper to different images, switch out the keyboard you use to type, and fully customize all the sounds used for different notifications.

Changing Your Wallpaper

Your Android tablet comes preloaded with a cool wallpaper. You can install other wallpapers, use live wallpapers that animate, and even use pictures in the Photos application as your wallpaper.

1. Touch and hold on the Home screen.

2. Tap the type of wallpaper you want to use. Use the steps in one of the following three sections to select your wallpaper.

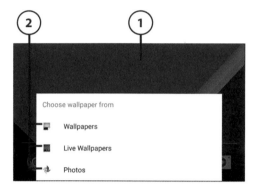

Wallpaper from Pictures in the Photos App

You can use any picture in your Photos app as a wallpaper.

1. Select the photo you want to use as your wallpaper.

2. Move the picture around on the screen so that it is positioned the way you want it. If you use your tablet in portrait orientation, keep it in that orientation when positioning the picture. If you normally use your tablet in landscape orientation, keep it in that orientation when you position the picture.

3. Use the pinch-to-zoom gesture to zoom in or out of the picture.

4. Tap the check mark to set the photo as the wallpaper.

Live Wallpaper

Live wallpaper is wallpaper with some intelligence behind it. It can be a cool animation or even an animation that responds to things such as the music you are playing on your Android tablet. Live wallpaper can also be something simple such as the time. There are some cool live wallpapers in Google Play that you can install and use, or stick with the ones already on your tablet.

1. Tap the live wallpaper you want to use.

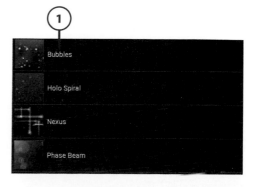

2. Tap Set Wallpaper to use the live wallpaper.

Find More Wallpaper

You can find wallpaper or live wallpaper in Google Play. Open Google Play and search for **wallpaper** or **live wallpaper**. Read more on how to use Google Play in Chapter 8, "Working with Android Applications."

Wallpaper

Unlike images from the Photos app, wallpaper images are designed to be used as wallpaper on your tablet. Your tablet comes preloaded with some wallpapers, but you can install more from the Google Play store.

1. Scroll left and right to see all the wallpapers.

2. Tap a wallpaper to preview it.

3. Tap Set Wallpaper to use the wallpaper.

Changing Your Keyboard

If you find it hard to type on the standard Android tablet keyboard, or you just want to make it look better, you can install replacement keyboards. You can download free or purchase replacement keyboards from Google Play. Make sure you install a keyboard before following these steps. Most keyboards your install provide a wizard to walk you through the following steps, but in case the one you chose does not, follow the steps.

1. Tap Settings.

2. Tap Language & Input.

3. Tap Current Keyboard.

4. Tap Choose Keyboards.

5. Tap the on/off slider next to a keyboard you previously installed (SwiftKey, in this case) to enable that keyboard.

6. Tap OK to change the input method.

Do Your Research

When you choose a different keyboard in Step 4, the Android tablet gives you a warning that nonstandard keyboards have the potential for capturing everything you type. Do your research on any keyboards before you download and install them.

7. Tap Current Keyboard again to change the default keyboard to the one you have just enabled.

8. Tap the name of your new keyboard to select it.

What Can You Do with Your New Keyboard?

Keyboards you buy in Google Play can do many things. They can change the key layout, change the color and style of the keys, offer different methods of text input, and even enable you to use an old T9 predictive input keyboard that you may have become used to when using an old "dumb phone" that had only a numeric keypad.

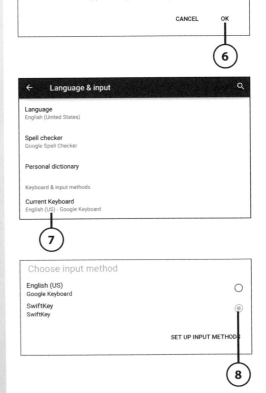

Adding Widgets to Your Home Screens

Some applications that you install come with widgets that you can place on your Home screens. These widgets normally display real-time information such as stocks, weather, time, and Facebook feeds. Your Android tablet also comes preinstalled with some widgets. Here is how to add and manage widgets.

Add a Widget

Your Android tablet should come preinstalled with some widgets, but you might also have some extra ones that have been added when you installed other applications. Here is how to add those widgets to your Home screens.

1. Tap the Launcher.

2. Tap Widgets.

3. Touch and hold a widget to move it to the Home screen. Keep holding the widget as you move to Step 4.

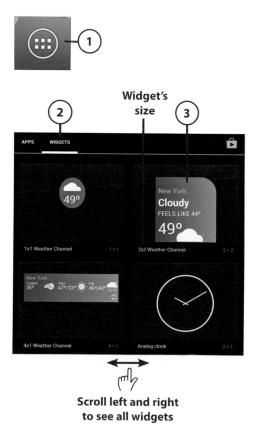

Widget's size

Scroll left and right
to see all widgets

4. Position the widget where you want it on the Home screen.

5. Drag the widget between sections of the Home screen.

6. Release your finger to place the widget. Some widgets require extra setup, so when you release them they may prompt you for more information.

How Many Widgets Can I Fit?

Each part of the Home screen is divided into four blocks across and four blocks down. Notice that each widget shown in the figure for Step 2 shows its size in blocks across and down. From that you can judge if a widget is going to fit on the screen you want it to be on, and the information also helps you position the widget in Step 3.

Remove and Move a Widget

Sometimes you want to remove a widget, resize it, or move it around.

1. Touch and hold the widget until you see a faint shadow of the widget, but continue to hold the widget.

2. Drag the widget to the word Remove to remove it.

3. Drag the widget around the screen, or drag it between the Home screen panes to reposition it.

4. Release the widget.

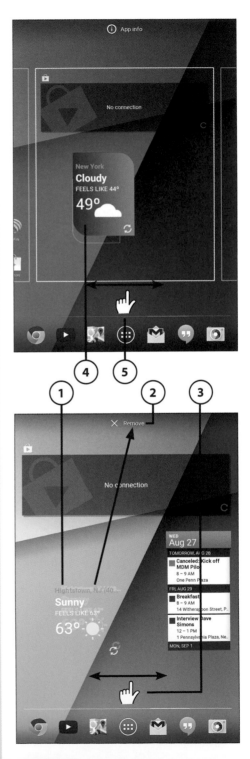

Resizing Widgets

Some widgets can be resized. To resize a widget, touch and hold the widget until you see a blue shadow and then release it. If the widget can be resized, you see the resizing borders. Drag them to resize the widget. Touch anywhere on the screen to stop resizing.

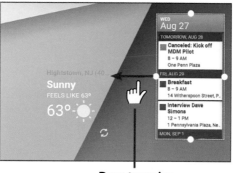

**Drag to resize
the widget**

Customizing Language

If you move to another country or want to change the language used by your Android tablet, you can do so with a few taps.

1. Tap Settings.

2. Tap Language & Input.

3. Tap Language.

4. Tap the language you want to switch to.

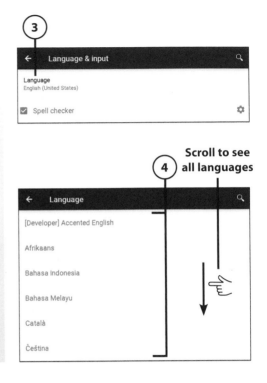

Adjusting Accessibility Settings

Your Android tablet includes built-in settings to assist people who might otherwise have difficulty using some features of the device. The Android tablet has the capability to provide alternative feedback such as vibration, sound, and even speaking of menus.

1. Tap Settings.

2. Tap Accessibility.

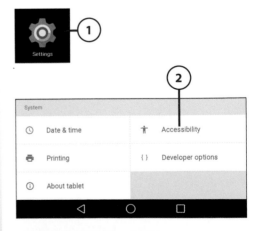

3. Tap to enable or disable TalkBack. When enabled, TalkBack speaks everything, including menus.

4. Tap to enable or disable Switch Access.

5. Tap to enable or disable Captions and how they look.

6. Tap to enable or disable the magnification gestures. When enabled, you can zoom any screen by triple-tapping the screen. When zoomed you can pan around with your fingers.

7. Tap to enable or disable large text. When enabled, all text displayed appears in a larger size.

8. Tap to enable or disable High Contrast Text. This feature is experimental right now but it makes text easier to read. For example, any white text will automatically get a black outline to make it easier to read.

9. Tap to enable automatic screen rotation. When disabled, the screen does not rotate between portrait and landscape modes.

10. Tap to enable or disable the feature that causes your tablet to speak your passwords as you type them.

11. Tap to enable or disable a shortcut that allows you to enable accessbility features using two gestures.

← Accessibility

Services

TalkBack
Off

Switch Access
Off

System

Captions
Off

Magnification gestures
Off

Large text

High contrast text
(Experimental)

Auto-rotate screen

Speak passwords

Accessibility shortcut
Off

Text-to-speech output

Touch & hold delay
Short

12. Tap to choose which text-to-speech service to use and what language it uses. If you don't want to use the Google service, you first need to install additional text-to-speech apps from the Play Store before attempting to select them here.

13. Tap to change how long you have to hold when you perform a touch and hold on the screen.

14. Scroll down for more options.

Accessibility

Services

TalkBack
Off

Switch Access
Off

System

Captions
Off

Magnification gestures
Off

Large text

High contrast text
(Experimental)

Auto-rotate screen

Speak passwords

Accessibility shortcut
Off

Text-to-speech output

Touch & hold delay
Short

What Is Switch Access?

Switch Access is designed for people with limited mobility. After you connect your external switch hardware via Bluetooth, you can enable and configure the Switch Access feature. You can teach Android to do certain things based on switch combinations. Read more about Switch Access at https://support.google.com/accessibility/android/answer/6122836?hl=en

Switch Access Preferences

AUTO SCAN

Enable Auto Scan

Time Delay
1 Second

Key Combo for AUTO SCAN
No Key Assigned

ASSIGN KEYS TO ACTIONS

Key Combo for NEXT
No Key Assigned

Key Combo for PREVIOUS
No Key Assigned

Key Combo for CLICK
No Key Assigned

Key Combo for LONG CLICK
No Key Assigned

Key Combo for SCROLL FORWARD
No Key Assigned

Key Combo for SCROLL BACKWARD
No Key Assigned

Key Combo for BACK
No Key Assigned

Key Combo for HOME
No Key Assigned

15. Tap to enable Color Inversion. When enabled your tablet uses the negative of each color that can help people with vision disabilities.

16. Tap to enable or disable color space correction for color blindness. After enabling this feature, you can choose the color blindness correction mode to use.

17. Tap to save your settings and return to the previous screen.

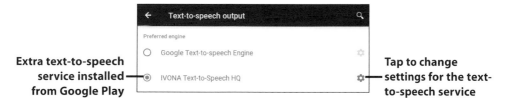

More About Text-to-Speech

By default your Android tablet uses the Google Text-to-Speech service to speak any text that you need to read. You can install other text-to-speech software by searching for it in Google Play. When it's installed, it shows as a choice for text-to-speech output.

Extra text-to-speech service installed from Google Play

Tap to change settings for the text-to-speech service

Modifying Sound and Notification Settings

You can change the volume for games, ringtones, and alarms, change the default ringtone and notification sound, and control what system sounds are used.

1. Tap Settings.

2. Tap Sound & Notifications.

3. Move the slider to adjust the volume for games and media such as videos and music, and ringtones.

4. Move the slider to adjust the volume for alarms.

5. Move the slider to adjust the volume for notifications.

6. Tap to manage your interruptions from notifications like messages and events, and whether you always want to be notified or only during specific hours.

7. Tap to choose what sound plays when you receive a notification.

8. Tap to manage whether to play sounds when you lock your tablet, insert it into a dock, or you touch the screen. You can also choose what audio is sent to your dock speakers (if you have speakers) when you dock your tablet.

9. Tap to choose whether you want your tablet's notification light to pulse when you receive an alert. This setting is only visible if your tablet has a notification light.

10. Tap to manage whether notifications are displayed on the lock screen.

11. Tap to manage whether notifications are displayed on a per app basis, and choose whether an app can send notifications when your tablet is set to receive priority notifications only.

12. Tap to manage what apps have access to the notifications. Some apps may need to have access to notifications so they can pass them along to external devices like Smartwatches, or Google Glass.

13. Tap to save your changes and return to the previous screen.

Device

⊙ Display | 🔔 Sound & Notifications

☰ Storage | 🔋 Battery

Sound & notification

Sound

🔊 Media volume

⏰ Alarm volume

🔔 Notification volume

Interruptions

Default notification ringtone
Tejat

Other sounds

Notification

Pulse notification light

When device is locked
Show all notification content

App notifications

Notification access
Apps cannot read notifications

More About Interruptions

You can manually manage how you are interrupted by notifications by tapping When Notifications Arrive and choosing either Always Interrupt, Priority Only, or Never. This allows you to manually set when you are notified. If you choose Priority Only, then you can choose what types of notifications you want to receive, and even who you want to receive calls from. Finally, you can set your Downtime, which is normally while you are asleep. When you set your Downtime, your tablet automatically switches to receiving only priority notifications during that time. This is great for when you go to sleep at night—your tablet will silence all notifications except for calls from certain people, and messages and events and reminders if you have them enabled.

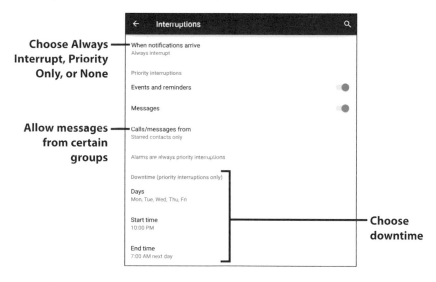

Changing Display Settings

You can change the screen brightness or set it to automatic, change the wallpaper, change how long to wait before your Android tablet goes to sleep, the size of the font used, and whether to use the Pulse notification light.

1. Tap Settings.

2. Tap Display.

3. Tap to change the screen brightness manually.

4. Tap to enable adaptive brightness. When enabled, your Android tablet uses the built-in light sensor to adjust the brightness based on the light levels in the room.

5. Tap to change the Wallpaper. See more about how to change the wallpaper earlier in this chapter.

6. Tap to choose how many minutes of inactivity must pass before your Android tablet puts the screen to sleep.

7. Tap to enable Daydream mode and choose what happens when your tablet daydreams. It can show the clock, cycle through colors, or show pictures from the Photos app.

8. Tap to choose the font size of all text used.

9. Tap to choose whether the contents of the screen rotate when you rotate your tablet.

10. Tap to use Miracast to mirror your tablet's screen on a TV or other device that has the Chromecast dongle attached.

11. Tap to save your changes and return to the previous screen.

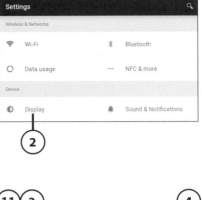

Changing Security Settings

The security of the data on your tablet is important. You may opt to set a device lock password or even encrypt the data that resides on your tablet.

1. Tap Settings.

2. Tap Security.

3. Tap to set how your tablet is unlocked. Your can choose Swipe (which simply requires that you swipe across the screen), Pattern Lock (which uses an onscreen pattern instead of a passcode), PIN (which is a numeric passcode), or Password (which is a password made up of all types of characters).

4. Tap to choose how long after your tablet goes to sleep (when the screen goes blank) it will lock.

5. Tap to choose whether pressing the power button immediately locks your tablet.

6. Tap to choose whether you want your owner information displayed on your tablet's lock screen, and what information to show.

7. Tap to enable and manage the Smart Lock feature that allows you to keep your tablet unlocked when it detects a particular Bluetooth or NFC device nearby, when it detects that it is in a specific location, or when it sees your face.

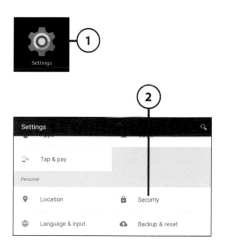

8. Tap to encrypt the data on your tablet. When you encrypt, unless you have a Samsung tablet, the encryption is irreversable. After your tablet's data is encrypted, anytime you power down your tablet and power it up again, you need to enter a decryption passcode.

9. Tap to make passwords visible.

10. Tap to manage Device Administrators. Device Administrators are apps that you have given permission to administer your tablet. One of the Device Administrators is the Android Device Manager. This enables you to log in to www.google.com/android/devicemanager on a desktop computer and reset your device password, or erase all your device's data if it has been stolen.

11. Tap to allow your tablet to accept apps not found in the Google Play Store.

12. Scroll down for more options.

13. The Storage Type item is for information only. It indicates whether your tablet supports storing your private encryption keys in the hardware (Hardware-backed), or if it is stored only in software.

14. Trusted Credentials allows you to view and select or deselect trusted credentials that the Android system uses, and the ones you may be using.

15. Tap to install certificates from your tablet's storage. This assumes you previously saved the certificate to storage.

← Security	🔍 ⋮

Screen security

Screen lock
PIN

Automatically lock
5 seconds after sleep, except when kept unlocked by Smart Lock

Power button instantly locks
Except when kept unlocked by Smart Lock

Owner info

Smart Lock

Encryption

Encrypt tablet — **8**

Passwords

Make passwords visible — **9**

Device administration

Device administrators
View or deactivate device administrators — **10**

Unknown sources
Allow installation of apps from sources other than the Play Store — **11**

12

Credential storage

Storage type
Hardware-backed — **13**

Trusted credentials
Display trusted CA certificates — **14**

Install from storage
Install certificates from storage — **15**

Clear credentials

Advanced

Trust agents
View or deactivate trust agents

Screen pinning
Off

Apps with usage access

16. Tap to enable or disable Trust Agents. Today there is only one Trust Agent called Smart Lock, but in the future there could be additional ones created by other software vendors.

17. Tap to enable or disable Screen Pinning, which allows you to "pin" an app so that the person using it cannot exit the app.

18. Tap to manage which apps running on your tablet are allowed to collect app usage information about all apps you have installed. This usage information includes how often each app is run, how long it sits in the foreground (active on your screen), and how long it sits in the background (still running but not visible).

19. Tap to save your changes and return to the main Settings screen.

More About Smart Lock and Trust Agents

Your tablet allows Trust Agents. Trust Agents are services you and your tablet trust are safe and you allow them to perform functions that override regular Android functionality. Today there is only one Trust Agent called Smart Lock. Smart Lock overrides your tablet's desire to lock the screen as long as it detects that you have a Bluetooth or NFC device close (for example, it detects your SmartWatch, you are sitting in your car, or you place your tablet on an NFC tag), you are in a specific geographic location, or it is able to recognize your face using the front-facing camera when you pick it up. To set up Smart Lock, tap Smart Lock as shown in Step 7, and follow the steps to configure either a trusted Bluetooth or NFC device, a trusted geographic location, a trusted face, or a combination of them to keep your tablet unlocked.

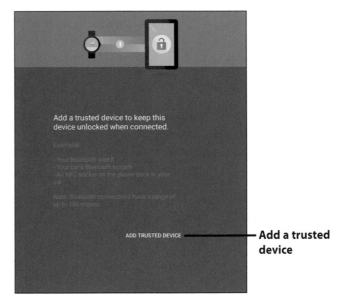

Add a trusted device

More About Pinning an App

When you enable screen pinning in Step 17, you are enabling a feature that allows you to "pin" an app to the screen. When an app is pinned to the screen, you cannot exit the app, go back to the Home screen, pull down the Notification or Quick Settings Bars, or do anything other than interact with the app. When you pin an app, you are asked whether you want to require a passcode to unpin the app. You can only pin the last app you ran, not any app. To pin an app to the screen, first run the app so that it is the most recently used app. Tap the Recent Apps button and slide the app up so that you can see the pin icon. Tap the pin icon to pin the app to the screen. To exit pinned mode, tap the Back and Recent Apps buttons at the same time. Pinning an app to the screen is a quick way to allow someone to use your tablet without letting them access anything else other than the app they should be using.

Tap to pin an app

Use gift cards   Send money

In this chapter, you find out how to set up Google Wallet on your tablet. Topics include the following:

→ Setting up Google Wallet
→ Using Google Wallet

Google Wallet

Your Android tablet has a built-in Near Field Communication (NFC) radio, which, among other things, enables you to pay for things such as groceries by holding your tablet close to the reader at the checkout counter. Currently in the United States you can use Google Wallet to pay for anything in stores where MasterCard® PayPass™ is accepted.

Download Google Wallet

Your Android tablet may not come preinstalled with Google Wallet. If it isn't, search for Google Wallet in the Play Store and install it. See Chapter 8, "Working with Android Applications," for more information on installing Android apps.

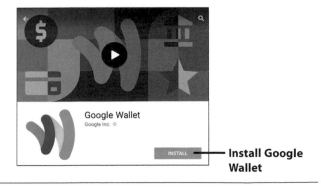

Install Google
Wallet

Setting Up Google Wallet

Before using Google Wallet on your tablet, you need to set a PIN to secure it.

1. Tap to launch Google Wallet.

2. Enter your name.

3. Enter your ZIP code.

4. Tap to check the box and agree to the Google Wallet Terms of Service.

5. Tap Continue.

6. Type a 4-digit PIN to secure the Google Wallet app on your tablet.

Wallet

Set up your Wallet

Legal name and current residence

United States (US)

Ford Prefect

☐ Keep me up to date with news and offers from Google Wallet.

☑ I agree to the Google Wallet Terms of Service and Privacy Policy.

CONTINUE

Enter Wallet PIN

editor.ford.prefect@gmail.com

○ ○ ○ ○

1   2 ABC   3 DEF

4 GHI   5 JKL   6 MNO

7 PQRS   8 TUV   9 WXYZ

0   ⌫

Adding Methods of Payment

Before you can use Google Wallet to wirelessly pay for items at the checkout counter, you need to set it up and select methods of payment. You may have already set up payment methods in Google Wallet if you have purchased items in Google Play. If you have, those payment methods are already available in the Google Wallet app.

Add a Credit Card or Checking Account

Perform these steps from the main Google Wallet screen to add a credit card or debit card as a method of payment.

1. Swipe in from the left of the screen.

2. Tap Cards and Accounts.

James Johnston
editor.ford.prefect@gmail.com

- My Wallet
- Transactions
- Wallet Balance
- Cards and accounts
- Loyalty and gift cards
- Orders
- Settings
- Help & feedback

3. Tap an existing payment method to edit it.

4. Tap to link a checking account to your Google Wallet.

5. Tap to add a new credit or debit card to your Google Wallet.

6. Tap to save your payment methods and return to the main Google Wallet screen.

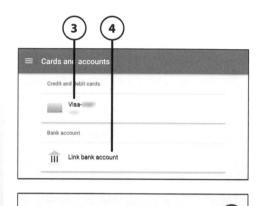

Setting Up Tap and Pay

Now that you have added your credit, debit, and checking accounts as methods of payment, you need to set up Tap and Pay, which makes it possible for you to tap your tablet at the checkout to pay for items. To enable Tap and Pay, swipe in from the left bezel and tap Settings. Tap on Tap and Pay. Google Wallet does one last check on your payment methods and then you're set. See the "Using Google Wallet" section later in the chapter to learn how to use Tap and Pay.

Using Loyalty and Gift Cards

Instead of carrying around your loyalty and gift cards, you can add them to Google Wallet. Once in Google Wallet, you can bring up the card at the checkout counter, and the cashier can scan the on-screen bar code.

Add an Existing Gift Card

Adding gift cards allows you to take pictures of the front and back of your gift cards, enter the merchant information, and enter your balance. This allows you to leave the physical cards at home. When a gift card is added, you get notifications when you are nearby a location where you can use it.

1. Swipe in from the left of the screen.

2. Tap Loyalty and Gift Cards.

3. Tap the plus symbol to add cards.

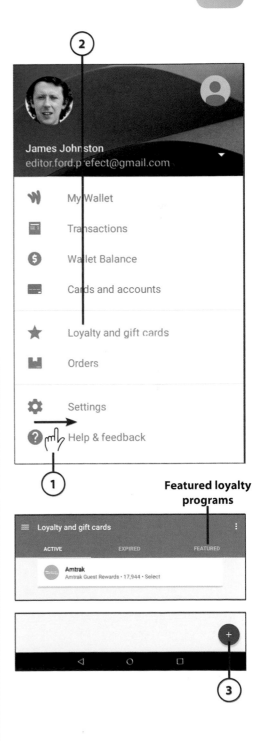

Featured loyalty programs

4. Tap Add Gift Card to add a new gift card. Google Wallet walks you through the steps of taking a picture of the front and back of the gift card, typing in your current balance, entering the merchant name, and entering your gift card account number.

Using Gift Cards

To use your gift cards, open Google Wallet and open Gift Cards. Tap a gift card to use. Google Wallet sets the brightness level on the screen very high and displays the card information—including a bar code for the account number—so that the store clerk can scan the bar code. If that option is not available, the clerk can simply read the information about your gift card on the screen.

Add an Existing Loyalty Card

You can add your store loyalty cards to Google Wallet so that you can use them at the store without having to carry around the actual physical reward card. After you add a loyalty program card, you can be alerted when you are near a location where the card can be used—and in some cases, your points balance can be automatically updated in Google Wallet.

1. Swipe in from the left of the screen.

2. Tap Loyalty and Gift Cards.

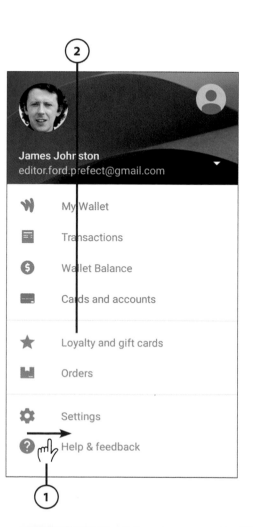

3. Tap the plus symbol.

4. Tap Add Loyalty Card.

5. Scan the back of your loyalty card. The screen will automatically advance once you align the camera angle and position so that the card is directly below and the edges are close to the corners of the scan area. Each scan area edge will turn blue once it is correctly aligned.

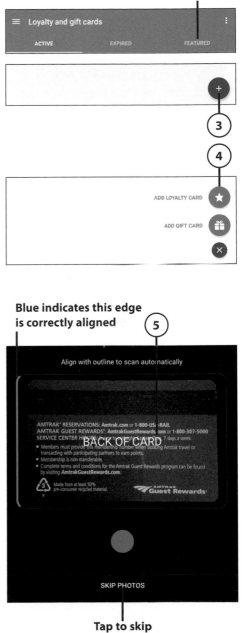

See loyalty programs you may want to join

Blue indicates this edge is correctly aligned

Tap to skip

6. Scan the front of your loyalty card. The screen will automatically advance once you align the camera angle and position so that the card is directly below and the edges are close to the corners of the scan area. Each scan area edge will turn blue once it is correctly aligned.

7. Tap Next to continue if the scanned front and back of your loyalty card look good, otherwise tap the Back button to rescan the card.

Tap to skip

Tap to go back and rescan

8. Type the name of the loyalty program and tap the name to add it. The screen will automatically advance. This example uses Amtrak.

9. Enter the name of the loyalty program. This example uses the Amtrak Guest Rewards program, so type Guest Rewards.

10. Enter the loyalty program account number.

11. Tap if there is a bar code on your loyalty card. When you scan the bar code, the account number will be automatically filled in.

12. Check this box if the loyalty card you are adding is not yours, but someone else's.

13. Tap to save your loyalty card.

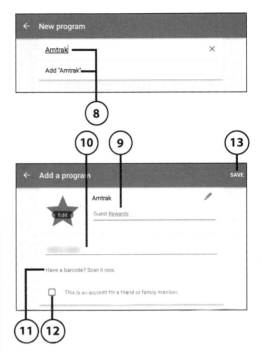

Using Google Wallet

After you have Google Wallet set up on your Android tablet, you can use it to pay for items at the checkout counter.

1. First make sure that you can use Google Wallet at the checkout counter by looking for the symbols shown in the figure.

2. When it is time to pay, press the Power button on the side of your tablet to wake it up (not shown). Some tablets do not require that you first press the power button to wake them up, and they will wake up when they detect the signal from the reader when you perform Step 3.

3. Tap your tablet on the reader (not shown) that has the symbols shown in the figure for Step 1.

4. You might be prompted to enter your Google Wallet PIN.

5. Remove your tablet from the reader after you hear the confirmation tone (not shown).

Google Wallet Settings

You can tweak the way Google Wallet behaves on your tablet.

1. Swipe in from the left bezel.

2. Tap Settings.

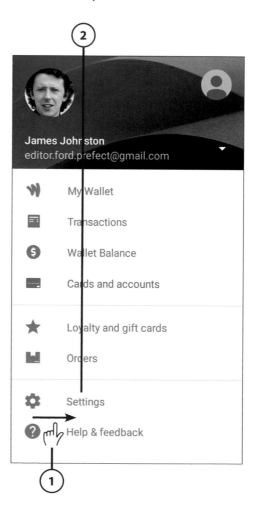

3. Tap to order a physical Google credit card from Google. This credit card allows you to use your Google Wallet Balance in the real world by just swiping your card.

4. Tap to set up Tap and Pay. You need to set up Tap and Pay before you can use Google Wallet at the checkout counter. Setting up Tap and Pay is simply choosing which method(s) of payment you want to use when you check out.

5. Tap to manage notifications from Google Wallet. You can choose to be notified when you are near a merchant where you can use one of your gift or loyalty cards, when there is an update to one of your gift or loyalty cards, or when someone sends you money.

6. Tap to choose whether you want to receive email updates from Google Wallet.

7. Tap to change your Google Wallet PIN and select how often you are required to enter the PIN. You can set the PIN timeout to 15 minutes, 1 day, or never. Setting it to 1 day or never is more convenient but might also be unsafe if your tablet is lost.

8. Tap to real-time order information for items you have purchased with Google Wallet.

9. Tap to view your monthly Google Wallet statements.

10. Tap to save your changes and return to the main Google Wallet screen.

What Is Google Wallet Balance?

Your Google Wallet Balance goes hand-in-hand with your Google Wallet Card. When you order a Google Wallet Card or you tap on your Google Balance, you are asked to verify your identity. Once completed, you receive a physical credit card that is tied to the Google Wallet Balance. You can add to the Google Wallet balance by transferring money from your existing bank accounts, or by accepting money sent to you via Google Wallet.

Sending and Receiving Money

When you have a positive Google Balance, you can send money to your friends and family using Google Wallet. If the person you are sending money to does not have a Google Wallet account, he will first need to set one up to receive the money. You can either use the Google Wallet app to send money, or if you use Gmail in a desktop web browser, you can attach money just like you would attach a picture.

Tap a book to read it

In this chapter, you find out how to buy books, read books, and subscribe to your favorite magazines. Topics include the following:

→ Buying books
→ Reading books
→ Buying magazine subscriptions

Books and Magazines

This chapter covers how you can use your Android tablet for reading books and magazines.

Books

The Google Play store has a section that enables you to purchase (and in some cases get free) books in eBook form. After you have an eBook, you can read it at your leisure and even bookmark your favorite pages.

Navigate the Play Books App

The Play Books app enables you to read your books, bookmark pages, and find and purchase more books.

1. Tap to launch Play Books. You will see the Read Now screen, which shows books you have recently opened and books that Google recommends you read.

2. Swipe in from the left of the screen.

3. Tap to shop for and purchase more books.

4. Tap to see books already in your library.

5. Tap to change the Play Books app settings.

6. Tap to the switch to see only books that have been physically downloaded to your tablet as opposed to all books you have purchsed, some of which may still be stored in the Google Cloud.

7. Tap to return to the Read Now screen.

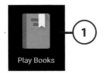

Play Books

James Johnston
editor.ford.prefect@gmail.com

	Read Now	7
	My Library	4
	Shop	3
	Downloaded Only	6
	Settings	5
	Help & feedback	

Buy Books

The procedure is the same for downloading a free book and buying a book. The only difference is a free book shows a price of zero.

1. Swipe in from the left of the screen.

2. Tap Shop to open the Google Play Store to the Books section. Bear in mind that at this point you are exiting the Google Play Books app and opening the Google Play Store.

Searching for a Book

Finding books in the Play Store is easy. You can swipe left and right in the blue area at the top of the screen to switch between different groupings of books—for example, Top Selling books, New Releases in Fiction, Top Free books, and more. If you tap Categories, you see books listed by categories such as Art & Entertainment, Education, Engineering, and so on. You can also use the search icon to find books. When you choose to search, remember that you can also speak your searches. One drawback of searching is that your search is done across all stores, so you see related results for apps, movies, TV shows, and books.

3. Tap a book to open it.

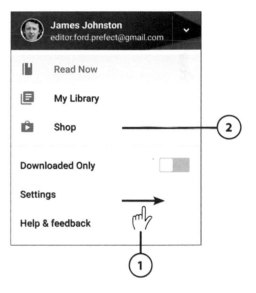

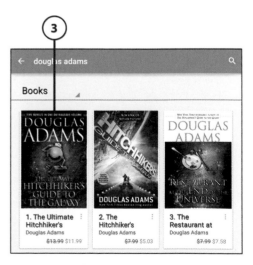

4. Scroll down to read reviews on the book.

5. Tap to read a free sample of the book before you purchase it.

6. Tap to purchase the book.

7. Tap to change the method of payment if you need to.

8. Tap to buy the book. The book immediately starts downloading to your tablet and appears in the Read Now screen.

Read Books

As you read a book, you can bookmark certain pages, jump to different chapters, and even change the font size.

1. Tap a book to open it.

2. Swipe left and right across the screen to flip forward and backward through the book.

3. Tap near the middle of the screen to reveal the formatting controls and controls for quickly moving to specific pages.

4. Swipe down from the top bezel or swipe up from the bottom bezel to reveal only the formatting and other controls.

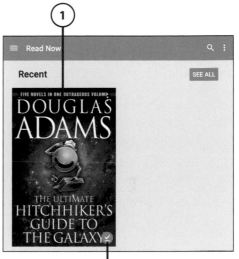

Indicates book has completed downloading

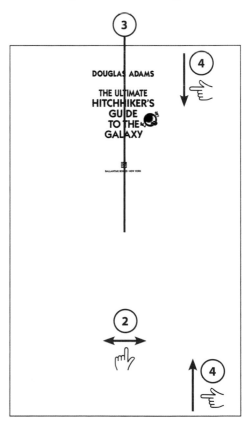

Jump to Pages Quickly

After you tap the middle of the screen, you can quickly move to specific pages in the book.

1. Drag left and right to quickly jump to a specific page.

2. Swipe left and right to skim through the pages.

3. Tap a page to return to the reading view.

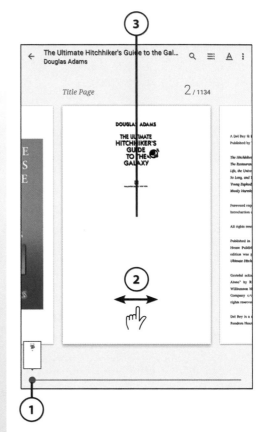

Formatting and Other Controls

After you tap the middle of the screen, or swipe down from the top bezel or up from the bottom bezel, you can control the way the book is presented on the screen.

1. Tap to search the entire book for a word or phrase.

2. Tap to list all the chapters in the book and jump to them, see notes you may have taken, and bookmarks that you previously set.

3. Tap to change the way the book appears on your screen.

4. Tap to see more options.

Control the Visuals

Tap the Font icon to reveal ways to control how the book appears on your screen. You can choose black text on a white background (typically used during the day), white text on a black background (typically used at night), or a simulation of real book paper color. If you are viewing the book using Flowing Text Mode, you can also change the typeface, text alignment, brightness, line height, and font size.

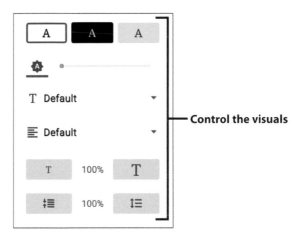

Control the visuals

5. Tap to switch between Original Pages and Flowing Text (if the book supports it).

6. Tap to share a link to the book you are reading via social media, email, and other methods.

7. Tap to add or remove a bookmark.

8. Tap to change the settings for the app.

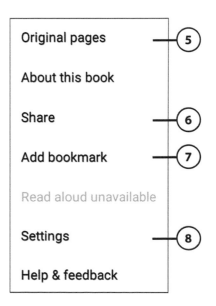

What Are Original Pages?

When you read a book on your tablet, the app defaults to showing the book using Flowing Text. This means that the text of the book is all there, but it's not structured in its original format per page. When viewing the book using Flowing Text, you can change the font, font size, alignment, and so on. Some books allow you to switch to Original Pages, which makes it possible for you to page through the book as it was originally laid out, using the original typeface and alignment.

>>>*Go Further*

TRANSLATING TEXT AND TAKING NOTES

As you read through your book, you might need a translation of some foreign text, or you might want to highlight some text and make notes about it. To do either, touch and hold the text you want to translate or make a note on, and then drag the markers left and right until you have selected all the text you want. Tap the appropriate icon in the toolbar.

Translate the text

Take notes on the text

Highlight the text

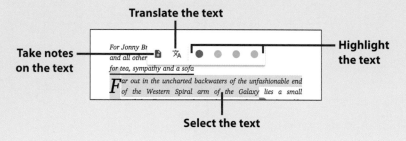

Select the text

>>>Go Further

SAVE YOUR BOOK TO YOUR TABLET

When you buy and read a book, it is downloaded to your tablet and stays there while you are reading it. If you know that you will be reading more than one book in an area with no Internet access (like on a plane), you should first manually download any books you think you will be reading so that they are available. In the My Library screen, tap the menu icon under the cover image of each book you want to download, and tap Download. After the book has been downloaded, a blue check mark icon appears.

Tap to download the book

Book already downloaded

Magazines and Newspapers

You can subscribe to magazines and newspapers on your tablet and have them delivered in electronic form to read anytime. The Play Newsstand app enables you to subscribe to and read your magazines.

Install Google Play Newsstand

The Newsstand app might not come preinstalled on your Android tablet. Before continuing with the following steps, please first install the app from the Google Play Store. See Chapter 8 for more information on installing apps.

Search for Stories

1. Tap to launch the Play Newsstand app. The first screen you see is the Read Now screen. This screen shows stories from different publications that you can read without subscribing to those publications.

2. Tap a highlight to read it.

3. Scroll down to see more highlights.

4. Tap to search for magazines and newspapers to subscribe to.

5. Swipe left and right to scroll through the categories of stories. Highlights are a mixture of stories from all categories, whereas all the other categories only show stories relevant to that category.

Purchase or Subscribe to Publications

You can subscribe to publications or just purchase a single edition.

1. Swipe in from the left of the screen.

2. Tap Explore.

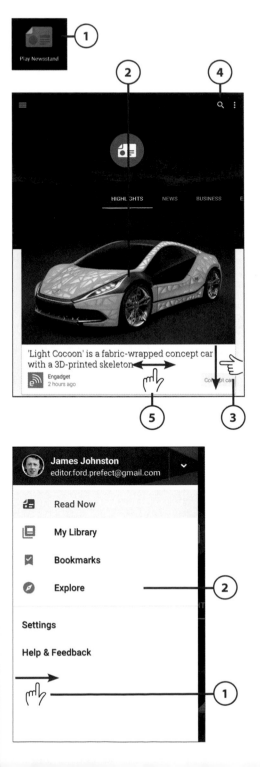

3. Tap a category. This example uses the Automotive category.

4. Tap a publication.

5. Tap Buy to buy just the latest edition of the magazine, or tap Subscribe to buy a subscription to the magazine.

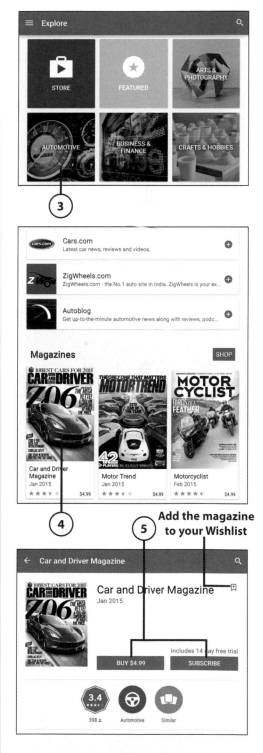

Add the magazine to your Wishlist

6. Tap Subscribe to complete the transaction. If you choose to just buy the latest issue, the Subscribe button reads Buy instead.

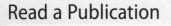

Read a Publication

1. Swipe in from the left of the screen.

2. Tap My Library.

Why Would I Download a Magazine?

When you open and read magazines they are temporarily downloaded to your tablet, but you are still required to be connected to the Internet before you read them. If you are going to be in an area with no Internet access (like on a plane) and you want to read a magazine, while you are still connected to the Internet you need to manually download it. To do this, tap the menu icon under the magazine's cover and tap Download. Once the magazine has downloaded you will see a blue check mark.

3. Tap the appropriate tab for the type of publication. This example uses a purchased magazine, which is on the Magazines tab.

4. Tap the publication to open it.

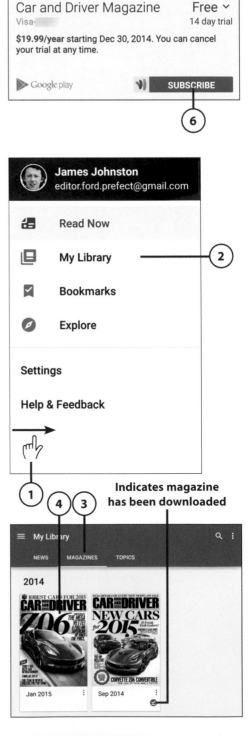

5. Scroll down to scroll through the article.

6. Tap near the center of the page to reveal the magazine controls.

Switch between page view and article view

What Is Article Mode vs. Page Mode?

If you tap the blue icon in the top-right of the screen, you can switch between viewing the magazine as it is laid out in the print version, page by page, or in article mode, which reformats the magazine so that you can move between the articles. When in page mode, if you tap on a page to jump to it, you can then continue to swipe left and right to page back and forth through the magazine. When in article mode, if you tap an article, you must scroll up and down to scroll through the article, and when you swipe left and right you can switch between articles.

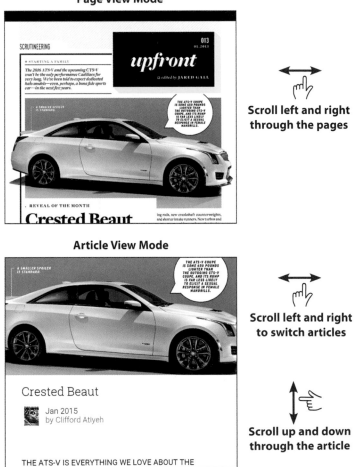

Page View Mode

Scroll left and right through the pages

Article View Mode

Scroll left and right to switch articles

Scroll up and down through the article

**See your battery
usage trends**

In this chapter, you find out how to maintain your Android tablet and solve problems. Topics include the following:

→ Updating Android
→ Optimizing battery life
→ Identifying battery-hungry applications
→ Caring for your Android tablet

Maintaining Your Android Tablet and Solving Problems

Every so often Google releases new versions of Android that have bug fixes and new features. In this chapter, you find out how to upgrade your Android tablet to a new version of Android and how to tackle common problem-solving issues and general maintenance of your tablet.

Updating Android

New releases of Android are always exciting because they add new features, fix bugs, and tweak the user interface. Here is how to update your Android tablet.

Update Information

Updates to Android are not delivered on a set schedule. The update messages appear as you turn on your Android tablet, and they remain in the Notification Bar until you install the update. If you tap Install Later, your Android tablet reminds you that there's an update every 30 minutes. Sometimes, people like to wait to see if there are any bugs that need to be worked out before they update, so when you choose to update is up to you.

1. Pull down the Notification Bar.

Manually Check for Updates

If you think there should be an update for your Android tablet, but you have not yet received the onscreen notification, you can check manually by tapping Settings, About Tablet, and System Updates. If there are updates, they are listed on this screen. If not, tap Check For Update to check manually.

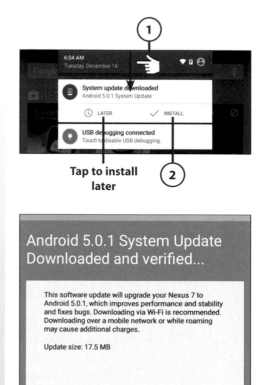

Tap to install later

2. Tap Install.

3. Tap Restart & Install.

4. Your Android tablet reboots and applies the update, showing you the status onscreen. After the update is complete, you will see the lock screen and you can use your tablet normally.

RESTART & INSTALL

Upgrade status

Optimizing Battery Life

The battery in your Android tablet is a lithium-ion battery that provides good battery life when you take care of it. Changing the way you use your Android tablet helps prolong the battery's life, which gives you more hours in a day to use it.

Looking After the Battery

There are specific actions you can take to correctly care for the battery in your Android tablet. Caring for your battery helps it last longer.

- Try to avoid discharging the battery completely. Fully discharging the battery too frequently harms the battery. Instead, try to keep it partially charged at all times (except as described in the next bullet).

- To avoid a false battery level indication on your Android tablet, let the battery fully discharge about every 30 charges. Lithium-ion batteries do not have "memory" like older battery technologies; the battery meter gives a false reading if you don't fully discharge the battery every 30 charges.

- Do not leave your Android tablet in a hot car or out in the sun anywhere, including on the beach because this can damage the battery and make it lose its charge quickly. Leaving your Android tablet lying in the snow or in extreme cold also damages the battery.

- Consider having multiple chargers. For example, you could have one at home, one at work, and maybe one at a client's site. This enables you to always keep your Android tablet charged.

Determine What Is Using the Battery

Your Android tablet enables you to see exactly what apps and system processes are using your battery. Having access to this information can help you alter your usage patterns and reduce the battery drain.

1. Tap Settings.

2. Tap Battery.

3. Tap to manually refresh the display.

4. Tap an app or Android service to see more details about it, including how much time it has been active, how much processor (CPU) time it has used, and how much data it has sent and received (if applicable).

5. Tap the battery history graph for more details on the battery history and how it relates to GPS, Wi-Fi, cellular data, and screen on time.

6. GPS On indicates when the GPS radio was being used through the battery graph's time span.

7. Wi-Fi indicates when the Wi-Fi radio was used through the battery graph's time span.

8. Awake indicates when your Android tablet was awake through the battery graph's time span.

9. Screen On indicates when your Android tablet's screen was on through the battery graph's time span.

10. Charging indicates when your Android tablet was charging through the battery graph's time span.

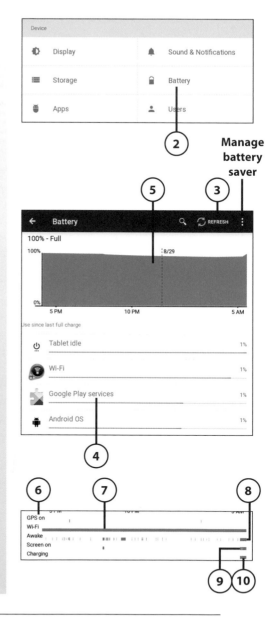

How Can Seeing Battery Drain Help?

If you look at the way your battery has been draining, you can see when the battery was draining the fastest, and you should remember what apps you were using at that time or what you were doing on your Android tablet. Based on that you can either change your usage habits or maybe come to the conclusion that a specific app you are using is misbehaving.

Applications and Memory

When applications run on your Android tablet, they all run in a specific memory space that is limited to 1 GB. (This number varies by tablet manu-facturer.) Although Android tries to do a good job of managing this memory, sometimes you have to step in and close an app that is consuming too much memory.

1. Tap Settings.

2. Tap Apps.

3. Tap Running to see only apps that are currently running.

4. The graph shows you how much memory is being used by the system (Android), apps that are currently running, and how much free memory is available.

5. Tap an app to see more information about it.

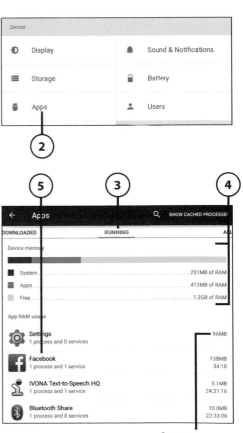

Apps memory footprint

6. Tap Stop if you believe the app is misbehaving.

7. Tap to report an app to Google. You might want to do this if it is misbehaving, using up too many resources, or you suspect it of stealing data.

8. Indicates the processes that are used by this app.

When to Manually Stop an App

After you have been using your Android tablet for a while, you'll become familiar with how long it takes to do certain tasks such as typing, navigating menus, and so on. If you notice your tablet becoming slow or not behaving the way you think it should, the culprit could be a new application you recently installed. Because Android never quits applications on its own, that new application continues running in the background and might be causing your tablet to slow down. This is when it is useful to manually stop an app.

Checking Your Apps' Data Usage

You might want to see how each app consumes data while it runs in the foreground or in the background. You might also want to limit an app's data consumption when it runs in the background.

1. Tap Settings.

2. Tap Data Usage.

3. Tap the date range to change it.

4. Tap a user or restricted profile to see total data usage for that user or restricted profile. This is useful if you share your tablet with others and each has their own user account.

Total data usage for the period

5. Tap an app to see more detailed data usage information for that app.

6. Tap to view and change the app's settings. Many apps have settings that control how they use data. So, if you think the app you are viewing is using too much data, tapping on App Settings might allow you to throttle its data usage.

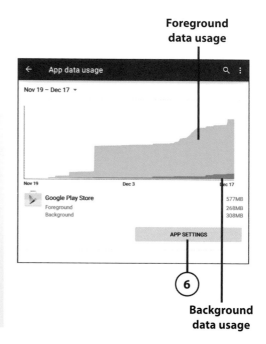

Foreground data usage

Background data usage

Caring for the Android Tablet's Exterior

Because you need to touch your Android tablet's screen to use it, it picks up oils and other residue from your hands. You also might get dirt on other parts of the tablet. Here is how to clean your Android tablet.

1. Wipe the screen with a microfiber cloth. You can purchase these in most electronic stores, or you can use the one that came with your sunglasses.

2. To clean dirt off other parts of your tablet, wipe it with a damp cloth. Never use soap or chemicals on your Android tablet because they can damage it.

3. When inserting the Micro-USB connector, try not to force it in the wrong way. If you damage the pins inside your Android tablet, you cannot charge it.

Getting Help with Your Android Tablet

Many resources are on the Internet where you can get help with your Android tablet.

1. Visit the Official Google website at http://www.android.com.

2. Check out some Android blogs:

   - Android Central at http://www.androidcentral.com/

   - Android Guys at http://www.androidguys.com/

   - Androinica at http://androinica.com/

3. Contact me. I don't mind answering your questions, so visit my official *My Android Tablet* book site at http://www.CraigsBooks.info.

Take panoramas

In this chapter, you learn how to take pictures with your Android tablet, how to store them, and how to share them with friends. Topics include the following:

→ Using the camera
→ Taking panoramic pictures
→ Taking Photo Sphere pictures
→ Synchronizing pictures
→ Viewing pictures

Taking and Editing Pictures

Most Android tablets have both front- and rear-facing cameras. The rear-facing camera is normally quite good, so taking pictures is not a disappointing experience. After you take those great pictures, you can share them with friends. You can also synchronize the pictures directly with your computer or using Google Photos in the cloud.

Using the Camera

Before you start taking photos, you should become familiar with the Camera application.

1. Tap to launch the Camera.

2. Swipe in from the left of the screen to change the camera mode between still camera, panoramic camera, Lens Blur, Photo Sphere, and video camera. (These modes are covered in more detail later in the chapter.)

3. Tap to change the camera settings. (See the next section for more information about the camera settings.)

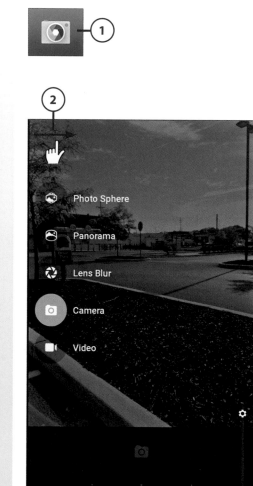

4. Tap anywhere in the frame to make the camera focus specifically in the area.

5. Tap to switch between the front-facing and rear-facing cameras, overlay a grid pattern on the screen, or manually adjust the exposure setting.

6. Tap to take a picture.

Zooming In—Is It Worth It?

Before you snap your picture or record a video (and also while you're recording a video), you can zoom in on the frame. To zoom in, place your thumb and forefinger on the screen and move them apart. To zoom out, move your thumb and forefinger back together. This is commonly called "pinch to zoom."

When you slide your thumb and forefinger apart to zoom in, the Camera app is faking the zoom. Although the image appears to get larger, what is actually happening is the image is simply manipulated to appear like it's zooming in. This is commonly called "digital zoom." Optical zoom is when the camera actually zooms using a lens movement, which is something that this camera cannot do.

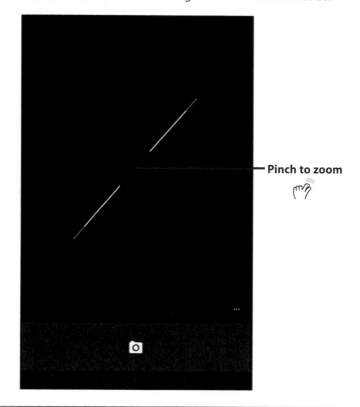

Pinch to zoom

Adjust Camera Settings

Using camera settings, you can change things such as the resolution of each picture, picture review time, filters, scene mode, white balance, and more. The settings that are not available when you're in video mode are noted in the steps.

1. Swipe in from the left of the screen.

2. Tap to see Settings.

3. Tap to enable or disable embeding your GPS coordinates into pictures you take.

4. Tap to enable or disable showing the manual exposure setting on the main camera screen.

5. Tap Resolution & Quality.

Photo Sphere

Panorama

Lens Blur

Camera

Video

Settings

Resolution & quality

Save location

Advanced

6. Tap to adjust the resolution and format of the pictures taken with the rear-facing camera. Your choices range from a 5 megapixel 4:3 ratio image to a 0.9 megapixel 16:9 ratio image. The exact range depends on your tablet's camera capabilities.

7. Tap to adjust the resolution and format of the pictures taken with the front-facing camera. Your choices range from a 1 megapixel 5:3 ratio image to a 0.1 megapixel 4:3 ratio image. The exact range depends on your tablet's camera capabilities.

8. Tap to adjust the format of the video taken with the rear-facing camera. Your choices are HD 1080p, HD 720p, and SD 480p. The exact range depends on your tablet's camera capabilities.

9. Tap to adjust the format of the video taken with the front-facing camera. Your choices are HD 720p, SD 480p, and CIF. The exact range depends on your tablet's camera capabilities.

10. Tap to adjust the quality of the images taken with the rear-facing camera when shooting panoramas. Your choices are High, Normal, and Low.

11. Tap to adjust the quality of the images taken with the rear-facing camera when shooting Lens Blur pictures. Your choices are Normal and Low.

12. Tap to save your changes and return to the main Settings screen.

13. Tap to save your changes and return to the main Camera screen.

Take Regular Pictures

Now that you have the settings the way you want them, take a few pictures. You can jump to Step 5 and take the picture, but you might want to first set up your shot. Remember to always take pictures in landscape mode for the best results.

1. Tap the Camera icon.

2. Swipe in from the left of the screen to change the camera mode.

3. Tap to select regular camera mode.

4. Tap the area of the frame you want to focus on specifically. When you release your finger, the camera adjusts its focus.

5. Tap to take the picture.

Focus on Parts of a Picture

You can actually focus on a certain part of a scene. By tapping the part of the picture you want in focus, you see that the rest of the picture goes out of focus. Using this trick enables you to create depth in your photos.

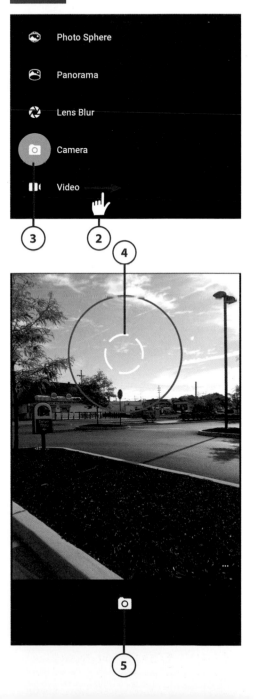

Take Panoramic Pictures

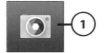

Your Android tablet can take panoramic pictures. Panoramic pictures are achieved by taking multiple pictures from left to right or right to left and stitching them together in one long picture. Luckily your Android tablet does all that work for you.

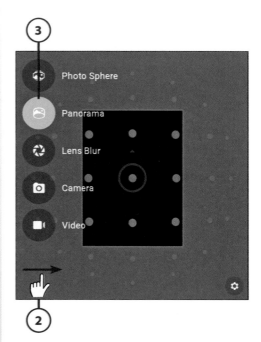

1. Tap the Camera icon.

2. Swipe in from the left of the screen.

3. Tap to select Panorama.

4. Tap to select the type of panorama you want to take.

5. Tap to shoot a horizontal panorama (left to right or right to left).

6. Tap to shoot a vertical panorama (up/down or down/up).

7. Tap to shoot a wide angle panorama.

8. Tap to shoot a fish eye panorama.

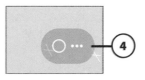

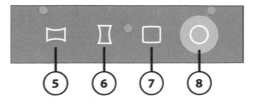

9. Tap to start the panorama.

10. Move your tablet until the circle is over the closest white dot. This is your starting off point. After the dot turns blue, more dots appear to guide you.

11. Slowly move your tablet around, and guide the circle over the blue dots. Each time you line them up, another image is captured for your panorama.

12. After you capture all the images necessary for the type of panorama you chose, the camera automatically stitches the pictures together into a panorama and saves it.

Can You Change the Width of the Panorama?

To create shorter horizontal or vertical panoramas, instead of rotating all the way from left to right, or up or down, you can tap the check mark icon to immediately stop the panorama process and save it as is.

Moving Too Fast

When you take panoramic pictures, you have to rotate slowly. If you start moving too fast, the camera indicates this to you. Slow down when this happens; otherwise the panorama will not look good.

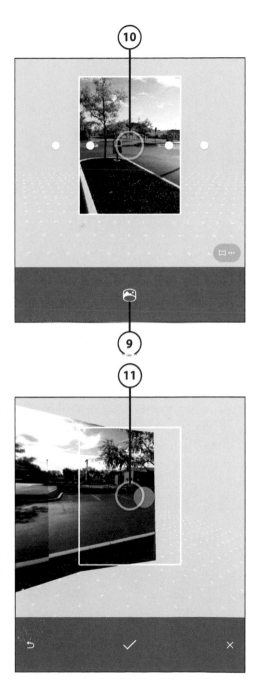

Take Photo Sphere (360 Panoramic) Pictures

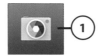

Your tablet can take 360-degree pan-oramic pictures—or, as Google calls them, Photo Spheres. Photo Sphere pictures are achieved by taking multiple pictures in all directions around you and stitching them together in one large sphere image.

1. Tap the Camera icon.

2. Swipe in from the left of the screen.

3. Tap Photo Sphere.

4. Move your tablet until the circle is over the blue dot. After you have done that, wait until you see other white dots appear.

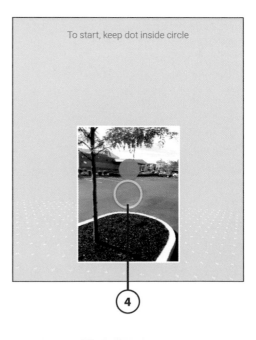

5. Slowly move your tablet around and guide the circle over the blue dots. Each time you line them up, another image is captured for your Photo Sphere.

6. When you have captured enough images, the images are stitched together in the background. You can view your Photo Sphere using the Photos app, which is covered later in this chapter.

Take Lens Blur Pictures

When you take a Lens Blur picture, you can change the focus of the picture after the fact.

1. Tap the Camera icon.

2. Swipe in from the left of the screen.

3. Tap Lens Blur.

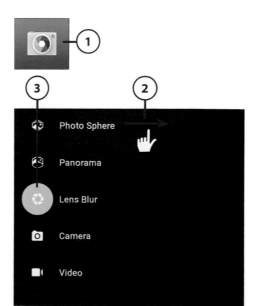

4. Tap to start the Lens Blur capture.

5. Slowly move your tablet up as indicated by the arrow.

6. After the picture has completed, swipe in from the right of the screen to see the image and adjust the blur.

7. Tap to edit the blur.

8. Tap the picture where you want it to be the clearest.

9. Drag the slider to change how blurry the rest of the picture appears.

10. Tap Done to save your changes.

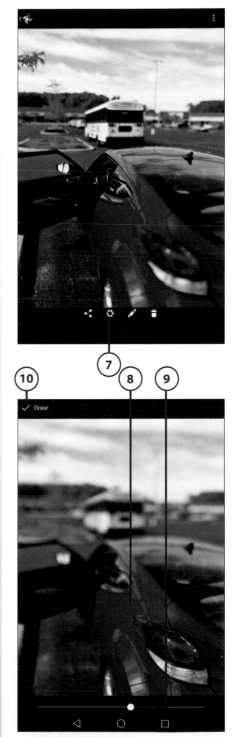

Viewing and Managing Your Photos

This section covers the photo-specific activities of the Photos app, such as viewing a Photo Sphere and editing photos. For more details about using the Photos app, read Chapter 2, "Audio, Video, and Movies."

Navigate Photos

1. Tap to launch the Photos app.

2. Tap to open a photo.

3. Tap to open a Photo Sphere.

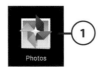

Where Are All My Photos and Videos Stored?

When you open the Photos app, in addition to allowing you to view photos and videos on your device, it shows you a lot of other options, so what are they? If you tap Google+ you see your Google+ profile. If you tap Photos you see all photos and videos on your device and also ones that have previously been copied to your Google Cloud account from this and all other devices you own. If you tap Stories you access a feature of Google+ that creates stories from photos and videos that have previously been copied to your Google+ Cloud account. Tapping Albums shows you all albums on your device and in the Google+ Cloud. Tapping Auto Awesome shows you any photos and video that have been automatically backed up to your Google Cloud account and turned into little movies. (You can also manually create them.) Tapping Videos shows you only videos on your device and in your Google Cloud account.

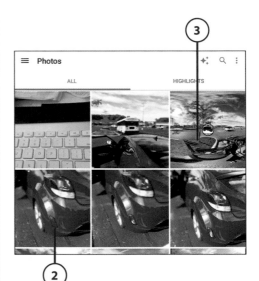

4. Swipe in from the left of the screen.

5. Select where you want to look for your photos, or just tap On Device to see only photos and videos you have recorded on this Android tablet.

Delete Photo Albums

You can delete one or many photo albums but only if they were created on your Android tablet. You cannot delete albums created on your desktop computer that you can also see on your tablet.

1. While you have an album open, tap the Menu icon.

2. Tap Delete Album.

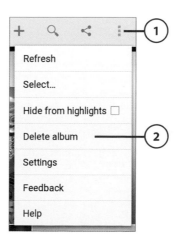

Review and Share Pictures

After you open a photo you can review it and share it with your friends.

1. With a photo open, double-tap the picture to zoom in to the maximum zoom level. Double-tap again to zoom all the way back to 100 percent.

2. Use the pinch gesture to have a more controlled zoom in and zoom out.

3. Scroll left and right to see all the photos in the album.

4. Tap to share the picture with friends using Facebook, Twitter, Gmail, Email, Google+, Picasa (Google Photos), and more.

5. Tap the method you want to use to share the picture.

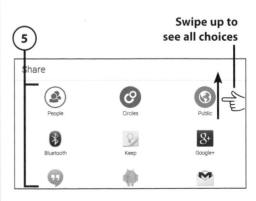

Use a Photo as Wallpaper or Contact Picture

While viewing a photo, tap the Menu icon, and choose Set As. You can choose to use the photo as a contact picture for one of your contacts, or use it as the wallpaper on the Home screen.

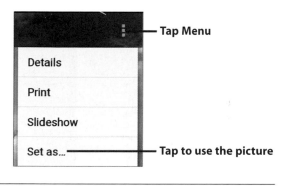

Tap Menu

Tap to use the picture

Can I Share a Photo Sphere?

You can share a Photo Sphere in one of two ways: as an interactive Photo Sphere where the viewer can move around your sphere interactively, or as a static image. Google+ is currently the only place that supports interactive Photo Sphere uploads. All other photo-sharing services and social networks, such as Facebook and Twitter, support only static images.

Edit Pictures

You can edit a picture by adding filters to it, enhancing it, or cropping it. These steps apply to still pictures, panoramic pictures, and Photo Sphere pictures.

1. With a photo open, tap the Edit icon.

2. Tap to let the Photos app automatically enhance your picture using changes it thinks will work best.

3. Tap to crop the picture. When cropping you can crop freely by dragging the crop box in any direction, choose to keep the original picture's aspect ratio as you drag the cropping box, or crop the picture always as a square image.

4. Tap to rotate the picture. When rotating the picture, you can rotate it freely using your fingers to make slight adjustments, or use icons to rotate it left or right.

5. Tap to add a filter to the picture.

6. Tap to fine-tune your picture by adjusting brightness, contrast, saturation, shadows, and so on.

7. Tap to do selective image tuning. This allows you to adjust selective parts of the image.

8. Tap to adjust the Structure and Sharpness of your picture.

9. Swipe right to see more picture adjustments.

10. Tap to make your picture look vintage.

11. Tap to add drama to your picture.

12. Tap to turn your picture into a black-and-white image.

13. Tap to enhance your picture to look like a High Dynamic Range (HDR) landscape.

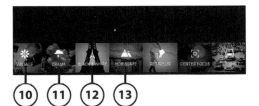

14. Tap to enhance your picture using the Retrolux enhancement, which makes your photos look like they were taken with old camera equipment, complete with light streaks and scratches.

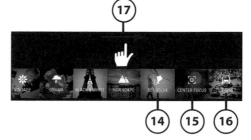

15. Tap to force focus on the center of your picture.

16. Tap to apply the Tilt Shift enhancement, which makes the objects in your picture look like they are miniature.

17. Swipe right to choose frames for your picture.

18. Touch to save your edited photo.

Get The Original Back

Even after you modify and save the picture, you can get the original picutre back. To do this, edit the picture, tap the Menu icon, and choose Revert. The original version of the picture is loaded and the modified version is removed.

Picture Looks (Filters)

You can apply filters to your picture to change the way it looks.

1. Scroll left and right to see all the available filters (or looks).

2. Tap a look to preview how it changes your picture.

3. Tap the check mark icon to save your changes to the picture.

Tap to cancel your changes   **Touch and hold to see the original picture**

Tune Image

You can fine-tune the image by adjusting brightness, saturation, and contrast.

1. Touch and hold on the picture and swipe up and down to see the different settings. Release when you see the setting you want to change.

2. Swipe left and right over the setting value area to adjust the setting.

3. Tap the check mark icon to save your changes to the picture.

Tap to cancel your changes

Touch and hold to see the original picture

Selective Tune Image

You can fine-tune different parts of your image instead of the entire image at once.

1. Tap the Add icon to add a tune point.

2. Drag the tune point to the part of your image you want to fine-tune. The tune point appears as a blue dot.

3. Touch and hold on the picture and swipe up and down to see the different settings. Release when you see the setting you want to change.

4. Swipe left and right over the setting value area to adjust the setting.

5. Tap the check mark icon to save your changes to the picture.

Tap to cancel your changes

Touch and hold to see the original picture ⑤

② ④ ③ ①

Tap to delete a tune point

Adjusting Structure and Sharpness (Details)

1. Touch and hold on the picture and swipe up and down to see the different settings. Release when you see the setting you want to change.

2. Swipe left and right over the setting value area to adjust the setting.

3. Tap the check mark icon to save your changes to the picture.

Adjusting Structure and Sharpness

To read more about the differences between the Structure and Sharpness enhancements, visit http://blog.phaseone.com/how-to-enhance-details-with-structure/.

Tap to cancel your changes

Touch and hold to see the original picture

Vintage Pictures (Make Your Picture Look Aged)

1. Tap Style to choose a style of aging you want to apply.

2. Tap Blur if you want to make your picture look blurry.

3. Touch and hold on the picture and swipe up and down to see the different settings. Release when you see the setting you want to change.

4. Swipe left and right over the setting value area to adjust the setting.

5. Tap the check mark icon to save your changes to the picture.

Tap to cancel your changes

Touch and hold to see the original picture (5)

Pictures with Drama

1. Tap Style to choose a style you want to apply.

2. Touch and hold on the picture and swipe up and down to see the different settings. Release when you see the setting you want to change.

3. Swipe left and right over the setting value area to adjust the setting.

4. Tap the check mark icon to save your changes to the picture.

Tap to cancel your changes

Touch and hold to see the original picture

Black-and-White Pictures

1. Tap Style to choose a style you want to apply.

2. Touch and hold on the picture and swipe up and down to see the different settings. Release when you see the setting you want to change.

3. Swipe left and right over the setting value area to adjust the setting.

4. Tap the check mark icon to save your changes to the picture.

Color Filters and Black-and-White Pictures

Because some colors look the same when converted to black and white, you can use color filters to correct this. Tap the check mark icon to save your changes. Read more about using color filters for black-and-white pictures at http://www.photographymad. com/pages/view/using-coloured-filters-in-black-and-white-photography.

Tap to cancel your changes

Touch and hold to see the original picture ④

Use Color Filters

HDR Landscape Pictures

If your picture is of a landscape, you might want to enhance it using High Dynamic Range (HDR) processing.

1. Tap Style to choose a style you want to apply (for example, whether or not your picture has people in it).

2. Touch and hold on the picture and swipe up and down to see the different settings. Release when you see the setting you want to change.

3. Swipe left and right over the setting value area to adjust the setting.

4. Tap the check mark icon to save your changes to the picture.

HDR Landscape Pictures

Read more about using HDR Landscape processing at http://www.lightstalking.com/getting-started-in-hdr-landscape-photography/.

Tap to cancel your changes

Touch and hold to see the original picture

Retrolux Pictures

Give your picture the appearance of being from film that has been damaged.

1. Tap Style to choose a style you want to apply. Tap the style multiple times to cycle through where the simulated defects should be added in your picture.

2. Touch and hold on the picture and swipe up and down to see the different settings. Release when you see the setting you want to change.

3. Swipe left and right over the setting value area to adjust the setting.

4. Tap the check mark icon to save your changes to the picture.

Tap to cancel your changes

Touch and hold to see the original picture (4)

(3) (2) (1)

Random defects

Center Focus

Give your picture the appearance of only being focused at the center.

1. Tap Style to choose a style you want to apply.

2. Tap Blur to choose if the blur is weak or strong.

3. Touch and hold on the picture and swipe up and down to see the different settings. Release when you see the setting you want to change.

4. Swipe left and right over the setting value area to adjust the setting.

5. Tap the check mark icon to save your changes to the picture.

Tap to cancel your changes

Touch and hold to see the original picture

Tilt Shift Pictures

The Tilt Shift effect makes the objects in your picture look like they are miniatures.

1. Tap Style to choose a style you want to apply.

2. Drag the blue dot to where you want the Tilt Shift effect to be applied.

3. Touch and hold on the picture and swipe up and down to see the different settings. Release when you see the setting you want to change.

4. Swipe left and right over the setting value area to adjust the setting.

5. Tap the check mark icon to save your changes to the picture.

Tilt Shift Pictures

To read more about the Tilt Shift effect, visit http://www.tiltshift-photography.net.

Tap to cancel your changes (2)

Touch and hold to see the original picture (5)

Modify Photos App Settings

1. Tap the Menu icon.

2. Tap Settings.

3. Tap to manage automatically backing up your pictures and videos to your Google+ account.

4. Tap an account to edit settings for that specific Google account.

5. Check the box to see photos and videos you have stored in your Google Drive Cloud account, in Google Photos.

6. Check the box to show the location of where photos and videos were taken.

7. Tap to manage how Google handles location settings for this Google account.

8. Tap to let Google automatically enhance your pictures when they are uploaded.

9. Check the box to let Google create "auto awesome" images, movies, and stories from your photos and videos.

10. Check the box to allow your tablet to do the Auto awesome processing.

11. Check the box to let Google recognize your face in photos uploaded to Google by your friends, and prompt them to tag you.

12. Tap to save your changes and return to the previous screen.

Managing Photos with Your Computer

When you connect your Android tablet to a computer, you can move pictures back and forth manually by using software such as Android File Transfer. If you have not yet installed Android File Transfer, follow the installation steps in the "Prologue."

Manual Picture Management

This section covers moving pictures using the Android File Transfer app if you use a Mac or the media transfer functionality if you use Windows.

1. Plug your tablet into your computer using the supplied USB cable.

2. Pull down the Notification Bar to reveal the USB Connected notification.

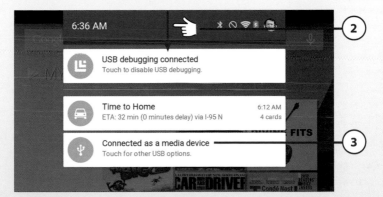

3. Tap the Connected As a Media Device notification.

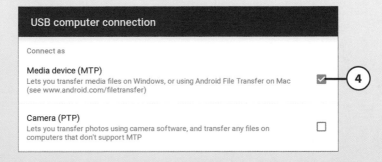

4. Tap to check the box next to Media Device (MTP) if it is not already checked.

Moving Pictures (Mac OSX)

After your tablet is connected to your Mac, the Android File Transfer app automatically launches, so you can browse the files on your tablet as well as move or copy files between your Mac and your tablet.

1. Browse to your tablet to locate the pictures.

Where Are the Pictures?

Pictures taken with the tablet's camera are in the DCIM\Camera folder. All other pictures are in a Pictures folder.

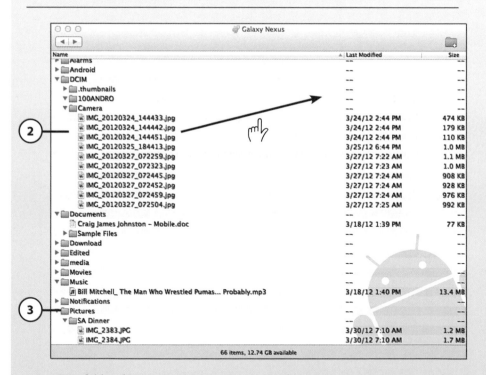

2. Save folders from your tablet to your Mac by dragging one or more pictures from your tablet to a folder on your Mac.

3. Create a new photo album on your tablet by dragging one or more pictures, or a folder filled with pictures, on your Mac to the Pictures folder on your tablet.

Moving Pictures (Windows)

After your tablet is connected to your Windows computer and mounted, you can browse the tablet just like any other drive on your computer.

1. Click if you want to import the pictures automatically.

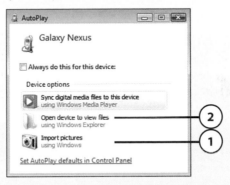

2. Click to open an Explorer view and see the files on your tablet.

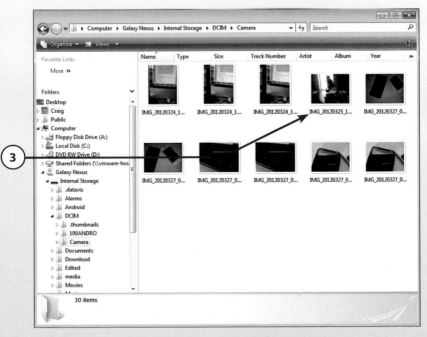

3. Save pictures from your tablet to your PC by dragging one or more pictures from your tablet to a folder on your PC.

4. Create a new photo album on your tablet by dragging one or more pictures, or a folder filled with pictures, on your PC to the Pictures folder on your tablet.

Where Are the Pictures?

Pictures taken with the tablet's camera are in the DCIM\Camera folder. All other pictures are in the Pictures folder.

Automatic Picture Management on a Mac

By setting your tablet to connect as a Camera, your Mac automatically opens iPhoto.

1. Plug your tablet into your computer using the supplied USB cable.

2. Pull down the Notification Bar to reveal the USB Connected notification.

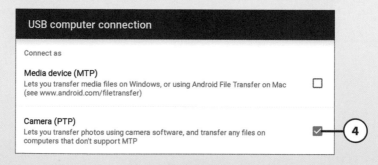

3. Tap the Connected As a Media Device notification.

4. Tap to check the box next to Camera (PTP), if it is not already checked.

5. Your tablet appears in iPhoto under Devices so that you can import photos like you would with any other digital camera. In this example the tablet is a Nexus 7.

Synchronizing Pictures Using Your Google Cloud

You can synchronize pictures to your tablet from your computer without connecting your tablet to your computer. Just use your Google account's built-in cloud service. All photo albums that you create in the cloud are automatically synchronized to your tablet.

1. Log in to Google with your computer. Hover your mouse over the menu, and click Photos.

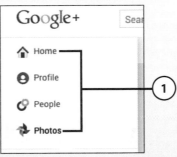

2. Download all photos from a specific day by clicking the down arrow to the right of the date and selecting Download.

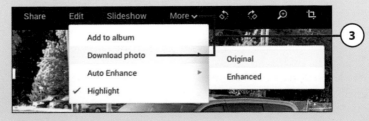

3. Download a specific photo by opening the photo, clicking the More menu, and selecting Download Photo.

Index

Symbols

3.5mm headphone Jack, 6
360 panoramic (Photo Sphere) pictures.
  See also panoramic pictures
  sharing, 305
  taking, 298-299

A

accelerometer, 7
accented characters, typing, 23
accessibility settings, customizing,
  236-239
accessing
  Google Now, 181-183
  previous/next websites in Chrome,
    164
  VPNs, 130
accounts
  adding, 41
    determining what to synchronize, 47
    first-time setup, 11
    Samsung tablet, 43
    troubleshooting contact
      information, 45
    work email account, 42-48
  Google accounts
    adding, 136-137
    multiple accounts, 136-138
    synchronizing, 138, 157

IMAP accounts, adding, 138-141
POP3 accounts, adding, 138-141
removing, 48
work email accounts
  adding, 142-145
  synchronizing contacts with, 42-48
ActiveSync server, 45
adaptive brightness, 242
address bar (Chrome), entering data,
  174
addresses, Wi-Fi and, 125-126
administration, Remote Security
  Administration, 46
alarms (Clock app)
  duration, 204
  managing, 202-203
  volume, 204
Album tab (Google Play Music app), 77
albums (music), filtering music by, 77
albums (photo)
  deleting, 303
  navigating, 302-303
alerts
  Calendar app, expanding, 209
  Google Now, configuring, 189
All Access (Google Play Music app), 75
Always-on VPNs, 132
Android
  blogs, 287
  updating, 279-280